MAKING GOVERNMENT WORK:
California Cases in Policy, Politics, and Public Management

MAKING GOVERNMENT WORK:
California Cases in Policy, Politics, and Public Management

Barry Keene, editor

The California Cases Project is Sponsored by
The Center for California Studies
California State University, Sacramento
Timothy A. Hodson, Executive Director
Barry Keene, Case Project Director

*These case studies were prepared by graduate students serving as Senate
and Judicial Fellows under the direction of The Center for California
Studies, which manages the Capital Fellows programs.*

Institute of Governmental Studies Press
University of California, Berkeley
2000

Library of Congress Cataloging-in-Publication Data

Making government work : California case in policy, politics, and public management /
Barry Keene, editor.
    p. cm.
Includes bibliographical references.
ISBN 0-87772-396-6
    1. Political planning--California--Case studies. 2. California--Politics and
government--Case studies. 3. Local government--California--Case studies. 4.
Intergovernmental cooperation--California--Case studies. I. Keene, Barry.

JK8749.P64 M34 2000
320'.6'09794--dc21   00-059712

CONTENTS

Introduction

I. The Executive and the Legislature

II. Local Government, Community Action, and the Media

III. Intergovernmental Dynamics

IV. Implementation and Oversight

INTRODUCTION

This is a highly condensed and somewhat modified explanation of the theory and rationale for using situational cases to help explain and improve public decision making. The more complete version can be found in the first edition of the casebook or downloaded from the web site of the Institute of Governmental Studies at the University of California, Berkeley at www.igs.berkeley.edu.

These casebooks are the product of an academic partnership between IGS, and the Center for California Studies at the California State University, Sacramento (www.csus.edu/calst). Editing and coordination hats, once again, are off to Director of Publications Jerry Lubenow of IGS; his Assistant Editor Maria Wolf; and Publications Coordinator Pat Ramirez. Thanks also to Ann Bailey, who joined me counseling students through the research and writing process, judging their presentations, and selecting cases. Finally, thanks again to the big guys for providing the encouragement, and especially the resources: Bruce Cain, director of IGS and Timothy Hodson, director of CCS. As I move on to yet another professional life,[1] I leave the case project in their capable hands.

They may not agree on what the essential skills are or on how to best achieve a command of them. A distinction is usually made between skills designed for use in a peer organization involved in collective decision making and those most often utilized in an administrative, managerial, or command setting. As in all human pursuits I can think of, there is an innate or genetic factor. Experience demonstrates, however, that it neither guarantees nor precludes success.

Public decisions are too important to be left to happenstance. The skills necessary to devise alternative outcomes are too important to be a product of trial and error. One cannot package them in a textbook in a way that does not deprive them of their essence. Those who have mastered them are too few and too busy to support apprenticeships. What remains? Here, wrapped in the art and power of well-told stories, are actual situations, each a delicate dilemma that requires a governmental response. In short, cases. As we explained in the first edition, California cases are used because of the state's

---

[1] Governor Gray Davis appointed me Director of General Services for the state of California effective mid-year 2000.

size, importance, uniqueness, diversity, and role as a trend setter. California is a crystal ball reflecting the challenges that confront our nation and the world.

The original research and writing of those cases was carried out by Senate and Judicial Fellows—graduate students enrolled in the Capital Fellows Program in Sacramento. Although an accurate recitation of events and description of actors were ever-present goals, characterizing conflicts will always leave some participants feeling that their stories were not adequately portrayed. We also risk complaints from advocates of competing policies that there was insufficient attention to the merits of their cause. We can only remind the latter that this is not about who was right on the merits, but how skillfully they advanced or defended their position, and how a final policy decision was made. Those pursuing idealistic objectives are most welcome; not to purify their idealism but to transform it into reality.

If this abbreviated introduction has encouraged you to look further, or enter the more advanced stages of case *writing* and *teaching*, you might want to download the full introduction. If you are still in doubt, read on. Or, do both.

Senator Barry Keene (ret.)
Director of General Services
State of California

I.　The Executive and the Legislature

Case 1

INTRODUCTION

Jim Gomez knew that the responsibility of the executive branch was to implement the laws passed by the legislature, with the governor's approval and sometimes, though rarely, over his objection. He knew that in California, there was an equal responsibility to enforce laws passed by the people through the initiative process. As a high-level appointee in the executive branch, Gomez took his orders from the governor and those higher up in the Wilson administration with respect to *how* his responsibilities should be discharged. He did not always agree with those orders, but he always tried to follow them as best he could. After all, it was Pete Wilson, not he, who had been elected by the voters of California. The most that Gomez could hope for in the event of a difference of opinion was that his opinion would be weighed and respected. When the decision was made, however, his duty was to uphold the command structure inherent in bureaucracy. A dependable, coordinated response is essential to the successful execution of the law.

Still, as an ethical and intelligent public manager, he must have wondered what he would do if asked to violate his principles. From what we know of his actions in this case, we can safely predict he would not have followed an order that he regarded as immoral. The closer question is what he, or any similarly situated administrator, should do when faced with a judgment by a superior that he, based on his own experience and professional judgment, regards as seriously flawed—even when the directive may not rise to a matter of high moral concern (although this one may have done so in Gomez's value system). When should the integrity of one's professional judgment prevail over the duty to follow directions and provide the dependability needed to sustain *a system of laws and not people?*.

From the standpoint of the superior, couldn't that question be asked of nearly any judgment to which some essential cog in the bureaucratic machinery takes exception? Where is the line beyond which the superior cannot reasonably count on an order being followed? Who is to decide where that line is? Can disobedience be tolerated, even once, without posing a threat to destabilize public organizations on which the entire system of laws rests?

Critics of the three strikes law, both as an initiative and as a legislative measure eventually in the same form, contended that its enactment would prove catastrophic: overcrowded prisons with a danger of riots; Scarce public resources used for unnecessary incarceration rather than crime prevention, or other more pressing public needs; Unfair outcomes for the justice system, with minor violations producing lengthy and sometimes life sentences.

Jim Gomez knew that at least some of the contentions were on target unless the governor, against his political interests, was willing to encourage a somewhat less strict version and encourage the legislature to pass it. Without the governor expressing a preference for a different version, there was no hope for something less problematic. In a general, but politically significant, sense the public was fed up with criminal behavior and ready to push penalties as far as they could. Supporters of three strikes seemed to expect that Gomez would use his professional reputation to support tougher penalties. Did he realize that his failure to do so would necessitate a major career change, if not a huge setback? Why, then, did he act as he did? Was it wise in light of the fact that he knew the more offensive version would likely pass?

Before you read the case, consider what actions you would have taken in the circumstances just described. Then, compare them with what Gomez did. Did he consider all the options open to him? On what basis do you believe he selected the particular course he adopted? When is a decision to follow public sentiment accountability and when is it cowardice? When is a decision not to do so foolhardy? Did most legislators feel it was best to survive the tidal wave of anticrime passions and live to fight another day? Did the governor demonstrate any sympathy for the views of Gomez?

Line Appointees: Three Strikes and He's Out!

Research and original writing by Senate Fellow Lucy Armendariz

THE GREAT PRISON STAMPEDE

In the decade that James Gomez had worked for the Department of Corrections, the state of California had constructed 16 new prisons. And after 10 years of increased sentences and harsher parole revocation laws the cost of operating the system's 28 prisons had ballooned to more than $20 billion. In 1993, when Gomez was named director of the sprawling system, there was still no end in sight. In fact, Governor Pete Wilson, his boss, had asked Gomez to endorse a tough new "three strikes" bill.

Gomez knew that if the controversial three strikes bill became law, it could raise the inmate population from 120,000 to well over 200,000. That, in turn, could require 20 new prisons at a cost of $21 billion. Staffing the new prisons could cost another $6 billion a year. Having come to corrections from a social service background, Gomez knew that most of those new inmates would need drug treatment and job training. A large percentage would have been incarcerated for nonviolent offenses, because that is what three strikes required. Excluding residential burglary as a third strike trigger, for example, would cut the cost of the proposed law by two thirds. Taking crack addiction off the strike list would save taxpayers $21,000 a year for each inmate incarcerated for addiction, as well as the cost of providing welfare payments for his or her family.

But, the lock-em-up, three strikes approach was attracting a growing base of vocal political support. To citizens fed up with the growing reports of increasingly vicious and senseless crimes, it offered a simple, direct, and forceful response. It would override the tendency, so the argument went, for sharp defense lawyers, soft-headed judges, and insensitive parole boards to free criminals to prey on a defenseless public. It was eminently exploitable by politicians who helped develop and then play to a terrified audience.

However unreasonable the grief and the anger that fueled the measure may have been, they were the byproduct of starkly dreadful realities. First, there was Kimber Reynolds. Then there was Polly Klaas.

CONVERGENCE OF HORRORS

Eighteen-year-old Kimber Reynolds had lingered in a coma for 26 hours before she died. The victim of a career criminal committing a robbery, she had been shot once point blank in the head. The next day, police ended the killer's career with 52 bullet holes.

When Governor Pete Wilson came to the Reynolds' Fresno home to express his regrets, Reynolds' father Mike told him, "I want you to know I'm going after these guys in a big way." He was as good as his word.

As chief sponsor of the three strikes initiative, Mike Reynolds turned his pledge into one of the harshest anticrime laws in California history. He persuaded Fresno area assembly members Bill Jones and Jim Costa to author legislation that would require 25 years to life for third-time felons. As insurance, should the legislature suffer a loss of will or courage to act forcefully, he also started collecting signatures for an initiative campaign. Indeed, the three strikes bill died the first time it was heard in the liberal-controlled Assembly Public Safety Committee.

Then one evening, several months later, 12-year-old Polly Klaas was playing with two friends in a bedroom in her Petaluma home when she was kidnapped at knifepoint. Her body was found abandoned in a field. She had been raped and slain by a previously convicted sex offender. Her killer, Richard Allen Davis, had just been released after serving eight years of a 16-year sentence. There was a nuclear-level explosion of public fury. Reynolds' three strikes office in Fresno was so deluged by phone calls that its electronic message equipment broke down.

Reynolds, and Marc Klaas, Polly's father, joined forces and convinced Jones and Costa to revive the three strikes bill. Legislators began tripping over themselves in a bipartisan rush to support it. On the verge of passing its final committee test, the deliberations stalled. Several senators wanted to amend the law to exclude nonviolent acts from being counted to invoke the mandatory penalties. Other legislators wanted to provide funds for crime prevention. Reynolds, incensed at the delay and possibly confused over why issues that he regarded as collateral were being raised, stood up and demanded to speak. "When we start adding amendments," he said, "it's

6

going to open a Pandora's box. It will demonstrate to me at least the inability of the legislature to act in a responsible way."

He could have stopped there; but he didn't. Reynolds went on to point out that the November elections were nearing. One of the senators protested that Reynolds' words sounded like a threat. Nonetheless, minutes later the committee rescinded the amendments. Even then Reynolds was taking no chances. "I understand this is a pretty slick town," he said. Fearing that lawmakers would find some way to undermine the legislative version of three strikes, he delivered the signatures for the initiative to the county clerks for a vote on the November ballot.

FATHERS' FALLING OUT

Then a disagreement developed between Mike Reynolds and the relatives of Polly Klaas over the best approach to take on three strikes. Their differences were highlighted when Polly's grandfather said it would be "a betrayal of Polly" if Wilson signed the three strikes bill.

When the Reynolds measure reached the floor, the grandparents sat in the rear of the Senate chambers quietly telling senators they opposed three strikes and supported a new bill by Assemblyman Richard Rainey that excluded nonviolent offenders but locked up for life those who committed a third violent felony.

Marc Klaas started talking to lawmakers like Rainey who were proposing alternative bills. Klaas realized that the three strikes bill as written would target not only murderers and rapists, but purse-snatchers and pizza thieves who would be placed in the same sentencing category as the monstrous Richard Allen Davis. To him, it diminished a level of punishment that should be reserved for the worst offenders.

Reynolds meanwhile was arguing that any proposed amendment requiring that a third strike be a serious or violent felony would signal a call for more "blood soaked victims." But Klaas broke ranks. He dropped his support of three strikes and became a critic.

The legislative analyst's office (LAO) estimated that three strikes would add at least $2 billion a year to the state's $2.7 billion prison system budget because it did not distinguish between violent and nonviolent crimes. The Center on Juvenile and Criminal Justice predicted that money for more prisons would have to come at the expense of cuts in higher education, law enforcement, and social service programs. If burglars alone were excluded, the cost of three strikes would be cut by two thirds, from more than $1 billion a year to $313 million.

Marc Klaas did not want to include nonviolent offenses in three strikes, and he began working the hallways and committee rooms of the Capitol. He felt used by the political system and resented hearing his daughter's name invoked in campaign speeches and commercials. He said that although he had once supported three strikes, he now felt it was flawed for targeting too many nonviolent offenders.

"All these people used my daughter's death to push their personal agendas, and that really upset me," he said. "When the governor came to Polly's funeral to make a speech, we were really flattered. But I think it was just to launch the three strikes campaign and his own campaign for reelection."

THE POLLY KLAAS SYNDROME

Many legislators returning in January after Polly's death were aware of the public outrage but favored amending three strikes to exclude nonviolent offenders. Mike Reynolds and other supporters would only accept changes that toughened the proposal. Shaking his head over the panic the pronouncement was causing, the powerful Speaker of the state Assembly, Willie Brown, said, "People are frightened; people are really frightened. Those kinds of horror stories wipe away rationality; it's very difficult to talk rationally in a crisis. You're talking about a group of people of zero courage. Not even Willie Brown, regardless of his persuasive powers, could alter the course. I would be shouting in the wind." Although he personally voted against three strikes, Brown made no attempt to dissuade his colleagues from supporting it.

It took courage for any California politician to argue that, as well intentioned as it might be, the three strikes measure under consideration was flawed and needed change. Brown thought Pete Wilson could have done it because his anticrime credentials were impeccable. But Wilson refused. In fact, running for reelection, Wilson announced early on in his campaign that he would make three strikes a cornerstone of his crime-fighting agenda.

A competing bill sponsored by prosecutors and police organizations and authored by Assemblyman Rainey targeted longer sentences on violent offenders, instead of nonviolent offenders like bad check writers, nonviolent burglars, or drug users. Prosecutors assailed the Reynolds bill arguing that

8

it would clog the courts, cost too much, and mean disproportionately harsh sentences for nonviolent felons. Prosecutors knew that the bill would increase the number of defendants who demanded jury trials rather than plea-bargain, straining the already underfinanced and overworked offices of district attorneys. Five district attorneys from around the state traveled to Sacramento to meet Wilson in his office and urge the governor to back Rainey's rival measure.

Senator Gary Hart, Chair of the Senate Education Committee, sought to exclude residential burglary from the list of crimes covered, thereby reducing the estimated cost by 70 percent. Health and Welfare Chair, Senator Diane Watson, wanted to have expressed legislative intent that for every dollar spent on the criminal justice because of three strikes, a dollar be spent on police, crime prevention, and drug treatment programs. Said Hart, "This is what a totalitarian system is about. Two burglaries and a bad check would trigger a life sentence. Is that consistent with what a democratic society is?"

Talking tough, Wilson made it clear that he believed burglars deserved life imprisonment: "The difference between burglary and robbery is whether or not you are at home. If you have the good luck to be absent when someone breaks into your home with a gun, it's your good luck you're not lying on the floor."

The Senate voted down the amendments by Hart and Watson, ignoring the arguments of other dissenters like Senators Lucy Killea, Quentin Kopp, and Milton Marks. "We allow ourselves to be driven like lemmings over a cliff by media driven frenzy," said Killea. "We aren't leaders." Kopp and Marks were among those arguing that Rainey's bill more closely focused on the problem of keeping violent career felons locked up.

Senator Lockyer quipped that Republicans are finding out "what Democrats have known for years: how much fun it is to just spend without any real discipline."

Assemblyman Phil Isenberg told his colleagues, "I've been here 12 years, and I've watched us pass a whole lot of criminal law stuff and I've voted for almost all of it. And let me tell you my impression. We don't have a plan. We don't have a theory. We don't have an approach. We don't have a program; we pile bill on bill, sentence on sentence. It is simply reacting. . . . hose of you who plan to make a longer tenure in public office than I will have to deal with the consequences."

9

CALL IN THE EXPERT

After the vote, the heat intensified on both sides. The media portrayed Democrats as soft on crime and described Republicans as fear mongers. To try to stem the flow of unexpected criticism, three strikes supporters sought the support of the experts. Jim Gomez, as director of the Department of Corrections, was called in to offer his perspective. Already in need of another prison to deal with the existing overcrowded conditions in his prisons, Gomez felt that correctional officers were increasingly endangered by the overcrowding in the prisons. Their union, the California Correctional Peace Officers Association (CCPOA), supported him. But, in contributing $51,000 to the three strikes initiative, they parted company with Gomez. CCPOA knew that more prisons meant more correctional guards and increased membership. They were quite content to have prisons filled with nonviolent offenders. Gomez was not.

Gomez had a difficult decision to make. As a loyal bureaucrat, he could testify on behalf of the administration of which he was part and defend three strikes as best he could. After all, the man who appointed him was chosen to be the chief executive of the state of California. On the other hand, he could give the legislature his best professional judgment—that three strikes was much too costly because it unnecessarily included nonviolent offenders.

EPILOGUE

Gomez decided to ask the governor to exclude burglaries from the strike provisions. The governor thanked him for his opinion, and Gomez left feeling he might have swayed the governor. But ultimately the governor signed three strikes without change, and Gomez decided to look for a new job: "I felt it was only going to get worse. There was no relief in sight. Ten years of bad laws wears on you. It was time for me to go." Gomez quickly found a new job as deputy executive officer for CalPERS, the retirement system for California state employees.

Several days after the bill was signed into law President Pro Tem Bill Lockyer told his constituents that those who supported three strikes, including himself, were a bunch of suckers. In a town hall meeting, Democrat Lockyer said he voted for the new law because his constituents told him to, but that it would cannibalize the state budget. Said Lockyer, "The public responded to the slogan 'three strikes and you're out.' It sounded good, and they think of these terrible Davis types who killed Polly Klaus. They think that's who they're incarcerating without realizing that mostly its application will fall on shoplifters and bike stealers."

Senator Leroy Greene, also a Democrat, agreed: "I'm going to vote for these turkeys because that's what my constituents want." Some Republicans were troubled as well. "Whether we can afford these bills, I don't know," said Senator Newt Russell, "but I don't know if we have any choice."

Meanwhile, Duane Silva, a 23-year-old from Tulare County sits in a prison cell serving 25 years to life. He was convicted of stealing a VCR and jewelry in a 1994 residential burglary. Silva is mentally retarded with an IQ of 65, equivalent to that of an eight year old. His first two strikes were for playing with matches, technically arson. One resulted in a fire in a trash can, another in a fire in a parked truck without occupants. The estimated cost of imprisoning Silva for life is $625,000. The Legislative Analyst's Office (LAO) reports that about 100 third-strike offenders are committed to prison each month. Most are committed for nonviolent offenses.

Pat Nolan, a former Assembly Republican leader, is known as one of the legislators who was toughest on criminals. After having been convicted of a nonviolent felony and sent to prison, he testified at a committee hearing, upon his release. Reflecting a change of heart, he advised his former colleagues: "We should lock people up who we're afraid of; not people we're mad at."

Joan Petersilia, a RAND criminologist says, "The legislature was not listening to sociologists, criminologists, or statisticians. It was listening to crime victims and the public's anger over two terrible killings."

The California Department of Corrections' Master Plan reported that the inmate population would exceed prison capacity in February 2000. Increasingly, offenders are asking for jury trials instead of plea-bargaining in three strikes cases, according to the LAO. Because of the increase in defendants in county jail awaiting trial, counties have had to release *sentenced* non-three strike offenders from custody. California's rate of imprisonment, 626 inmates for every 100,000 residents, is 21 percent higher than the rate for the rest of the United States. Indeed, if California were a nation, its incarceration rate and violent crime rate would lead the world.

Case 2

INTRODUCTION

From Where the Power Flows provides insights into the hardball politics of the budget process. It occurs just as an environment of scarce public revenues finally begins an economically prosperous transformation. The lengthy recession, however, has provided ostensible justification for a process in which the Big Five leaders had commandeered the budget process. Their extraordinary powers, embodied in the relationships among them had attained institutional status. Compare it with the current environment in which huge revenue surpluses have appeared. What effect should the much improved economy have on the rationale supporting the Big Five?

It is argued that *term limits* will require a greater concentration of power in the leadership to get things accomplished. With the rationale for the Big Five withering, won't the very opposite occur? Consider, in reading the case, the effect of the *supermajority* requirement for passage of the budget. For example, would even the Republican governor have been better off if the requirement had only been a simple majority—thus eliminating the necessity of pleasing the two Republican leaders?

Consider the effect of *divided government*—a Democratic legislative majority and a Republican governor—on the politics of the situation.

If term limits makes members less willing to sacrifice a short-term advantage—a tax cut for Republicans or more spending for Democrats—for long-term interests that do not afford political benefits, what does this explain about some of the leadership positions taken? Are their interests necessarily the same as the members of their own caucuses? What made the governor believe he was in a powerful enough position to get Democrats to agree to a tax reduction? Senator Hurtt seemed to feel that an immediate payback, in terms of the public interest, was every bit as good as, maybe better than, a tax cut. However, he candidly admitted that the latter was better politics and would probably prevail. Were you surprised by his candor? Did the governor miscalculate and feel he was bluffing?

Consider the anomaly that permits tax cuts to occur with a simple majority vote, but requires a two-thirds vote to eliminate tax advantages for specified interests. Does that make tax loopholes effectively irreversible? What effect would term limits have on the will to resist irreversible tax cuts? Would the governor have been in a stronger position if the Big Five had not been in control—if there were a more inclusionary process? Could he have divided Democratic members from their leaders?

Did both caucuses miscalculate the governor's willingness to use his "neutron bomb"? He was not a person whose history supported the frequent use of "bluffing." Among the key players, who were the winners and who were the losers? This is a case of hardball politics at its hardest!

The Big Five: From Where the Power Flows

Research and original writing by Senate Fellow Jason Hughes

THE CALM BEFORE . . .

With the economy booming, unemployment at a six-year low, and the tax coffers brimming with a $2.3 billion surplus, adopting California's 1997-98 state budget should have been relatively easy. One of the most controversial issues in recent years had finally been put to bed in what seemed like a miraculous bipartisan compromise. The federal Welfare Reform Act adopted in 1996 required sweeping changes in California's welfare policy. Passage of Assembly Bill 1542 created California Work Opportunity and Responsibility to Kids (CalWORKS) and replaced AFDC. Billed as a split-the-difference compromise, it imposed a five-year lifetime limit for recipients and demanded that they work or be involved in job training while receiving benefits.

Money for the new programs was to be provided in the budget. It was a lot but it was there. According to Senator Rob Hurtt, the Senate Minority Leader, "Welfare reform had been responsible for ¾ of the budget delay." Said Assembly Minority Leader Curt Pringle, "The welfare portion of the budget was almost 30 percent of the money. You couldn't deal with the rest of the budget until you dealt with welfare." Senate President Pro Tempore Bill Lockyer agreed, "Welfare reform had been a major sticking point in negotiating the budget."

Knowing that food stamps for legal immigrants was a divisive issue, Democratic Assembly Speaker Cruz Bustamante put controversial nonfiscal items of welfare reform implementation into bills that would need only a simple majority to pass each house.[1] Thus, the largest impediment to enacting a new state budget—welfare reform—was miraculously removed. Even the two-thirds vote of each house required to pass the budget did not seem so difficult a hurdle.

... THE STORM

Then, a dramatic development resulted in the second longest budget impasse in California's history and a political battle never to be forgotten. The California Supreme Court affirmed the unconstitutionality of past years' deferrals of $1.36 billion in state contributions to the California Public Employees' Retirement System (PERS). It was due and payable with more billions in compound interest continuing to accumulate on a frighteningly large daily basis.

Before 1990, the state made its retirement contributions monthly. With a shrinking budget, due to the beginning of a recession, the legislature decided in 1990 to change the payment schedule from monthly to quarterly. Regarded as a quick, painless, and temporary fix, it helped that year to meet the constitutional requirement for a balanced budget. The following year, the payment schedule was changed from quarterly to semi-annually. The year after, payments were not made until the state was six months in arrears. Finally, in 1993, it was agreed that payments would be made annually, after the state fell into arrears for a year. These were more than book keeping changes. They resulted in a reduction of the money available to PERS for investment. The state began floating hundreds of millions of dollars that were earning interest that seemingly belonged to state employees.

With more than $129 billion in assets, covering more than 2,400 employers, PERS provides retirement and health benefits to more than a million state and local public employees, retirees, and their families and beneficiaries. Membership is divided approximately in thirds among current and former employees of the state, schools, and participating public agencies. PERS and the state employee unions took the state of California to court. Around Christmas of 1994, their gift was a lower court ruling that the state's actions were illegal. The judge ordered the administration to forward the

---

[1]Mark Barabak, "Cruz Bustamante on Surviving a Bruising First Term as Assembly Speaker, *Los Angeles Times*, A-3, August 24, 1997.

withheld money to the pension trust with an additional 8 ¾ percent interest. Said Judge John Lewis of Sacramento: "[If the court failed to order repayment] . . . it would be an invitation . . . to continue to relieve the fiscal constraints of these difficult economic times in this manner." In early 1996, the Court of Appeal decided 3-0 to uphold Lewis' ruling. With the May decision by the Supreme Court, a shocked governor and legislature thought it self-evident that it would be impossible politically to make the repayment in a single year, because it would kill expectations for legislative and executive augmentations to the budget. They decided repayment simply would have to be spread out over a number of years. According to Senator Hurtt, the court's decision had a dramatic impact on the legislature and budget negotiations: "Immediately we were faced with some tough decisions. Everyone had his or her hand in the cookie jar, and it became pretty evident that not everyone was going to be fed."

THE BIG 5

In January of every year, the governor presents his budget proposal to the legislature. Then, budget committees in each house of the legislature review and amend the proposal to suit their agendas. Perceptions of the current method of the budget process vary. According to Senator Hurtt, "The budget committee process is somewhat of a sham. The Senate makes a budget and the Assembly makes a budget, and who ever is in control comes up with their kind of budget. Then they go to joint committee and reconcile the two, and it comes out in the end as totally the majority party's budget, which is far removed from the governor's ideas, or anything that the Republican members would vote for. . . . They have to have our votes to pass it."

"As a general matter, the governor gets it his way," said Lockyer, "because . . . of the 2/3 vote, the veto, and the line item veto the strength belongs to the him." The committee process becomes all the more difficult in years where there is a budget surplus. When you have open meetings, "All of the special interest groups get up there with their hands out and start complaining."

In the late nineties, the failure of the prescribed mechanisms to pass an agreeable budget led to empowerment of "the Big 5"—the governor and the majority and minority leaders of both houses. Governor Wilson, Senator Lockyer, Senator Hurtt, Assemblyman Bustamante, and Assemblyman

Pringle were the players on this occasion. While the Conference Committee's public meetings were on hold, or they ironed out minor matters, the Big 5 met behind closed doors. Said Lockyer:

> It's a device, process, procedure that allows complicated issues to come to closure when there are significant disagreements between the parties. You can't have the state budget adopted by 32 million people. You have to figure out a practical way to let those general viewpoints and policy currents reach the capital through the elected representatives. And once you're here, there are 120 different opinions. Rarely is there a topic that legislators are sufficiently in agreement with to achieve the 2/3-vote necessary. Especially on complicated matters like the budget.

Assemblyman Curt Pringle agreed. "We would all come to the table and throw all of our demands out. We would then pick the things we thought the money should go to. After that we would take it back to the caucus and sell it to our members." It would be impossible to please all of the members. Not everyone got what he or she wanted: "There would be times when we would come in and say, this park is very important to Senator X. I would like the record to reflect that I fought hard to get it, and then we would all just move on."

The future of the Big 5 is uncertain. "If anything, term limits will decrease the power of the Big 5. Leaders won't have as much pull with their caucuses and may not be able to sell the outcomes as well. There was never any doubt that when Willie Brown said he would do a deal, that it was done," said Pringle.

Lockyer disagreed: "It's here; the Big 5 is an institution which has been used extensively by this governor, and I'm sure it will be used by the governors to come."

RUNNING THEM THROUGH THE SOFT SAND

The Big 5 is not necessarily an easy answer to solving the budget problems. According to Lockyer, "There is a certain rhythm to negotiations. In this case the governor didn't seem eager to close." More than one member of the Big 5 had comments on Wilson's negotiating strategy. "He has an expression," said Lockyer, "for people who aren't ready to adopt his view. He describes it as 'running them through the soft sand' to wear them out."

Said Hurtt, "He'll kind of numb everybody to death, and finally they'll come to an agreement. It's much harder on the rest of the leadership because they all have to travel back and forth. It became very strenuous."

In 1997, Pringle and Hurtt sat down a number of times with the governor to find out what the leadership wanted. And Wilson was clearly the point man for the Republicans. "The Republican legislative leaders don't have much of a role. It's either the governor's deal or nothing," said Hurtt.

We weren't getting much. We wanted a decrease [in taxes] throughout the whole year. First, we went to him back in the spring and he said, 'No it won't fly.' Then as we got closer he said, 'Well maybe it will but I don't want to do anything for public consumption because the CTA will have plenty of time, and they will start beating us up.' There may be some validity to that, but I don't think it's as much as he thinks. He just didn't want them to know what his plan was. The problem was, he didn't let us know what his plan was either.

I would have preferred to sit with the governor and come to an agreement among the three of us. That would have been the most logical thing. Let him negotiate with us a little bit and give us something to satisfy our caucus. We all have different personalities and different things that we are trying to get done. The minority leaders become the salesmen. We go back and we are supposed to report and convince our members of the decisions we have made. Meanwhile you go to meeting after meeting after meeting. They last between 2-3 hours a meeting, and you only talk about something meaningful about 50 percent of time.

The largest political issue faced by the Big 5 was how to repay the CalPERS settlement. Should the repayment be in one lump sum or spread out over as many as 10 years?

PERS-PECTIVE

"CalPERS had won the lawsuit," said Jim Gomez, Deputy Executive Officer of CalPERS.[6] "We were going to get the $1.3 billion one way or the other, either through getting a court order for them to deliver the money to us, or some agreement on how it would be paid back." The unions saw the PERS repayment as a way to force the governor to negotiate contracts for state workers. According to Cathy Hackett, the deputy director of the California State Employees Association (CSEA), "We were extensively involved with the meetings on the repayment plan. We had many concerns in the retirement area because our members were all in the two-tier retirement system. That system wasn't paying a living wage."[2]

Jim Hard, director of the CSEA said, "Part of the repayment plan was a derived benefit. If the governor chose to pay back the debt in payments, you have to give some kind of derived benefit to the people of the PERS system."[3]

"The issue of (unions) making demands on the governor for raises had nothing to do with us." said Gomez. "We are only responsible for retirement here. They could have used the money to pay for a share of retirement benefits, but their demands for a three percent wage increase were not considered in our negotiations."

At the bargaining table, CSEA's nine bargaining teams continued to meet with the Department of Finance to come up with a solution that would benefit state employees. Jim Hard did his best to turn up the heat on the governor: "The union was asking the legislature not to agree to any budget until we reach fair contract settlements with the Wilson administration."

"Thousands of state employees showed up for the June 27 Capitol rally," explained Hackett. Our slogan was "Recognize state workers with raises, rights, respect, or we will hold up the budget. We will stop it."

> As it turns out, we were only a small part of the political scene. At the end of the session, it came down to several big issues, the tax cut, education, welfare, and our contract. The proposal was that there wouldn't be a deal on the tax cut until we got a deal on our contracts. Ultimately the unions didn't have the clout with the Republicans or Democrats. Neither side wanted to face an election year where the governor could say he put forth a large tax cut and they failed to compromise on it. Especially with such a large surplus. Unfortunately for us, we weren't strong enough to be a part of that inner compromise. In the end, I think we got left out. It was a sobering experience.

"The unions were a paper tiger," said a member of the Republican leadership. "I was with Wilson one day when they were picketing the driveways in the basement, and he pointed at them and said 'Look at those

---

[2]Interview Cathy Hackett, CSEA 500, March 5, 1998.
[3]Interview Jim Hard, CSEA 500, March 5, 1998.

suckers out there.' They put up every penny against him in his election, so he didn't have much sympathy for them. Why should he give them a pay increase so that they could give more money to their unions to try and beat Republicans and elect Democrats?"

CalPERS conducted a series of six meetings with the Department of Finance to decide how to go about repaying the debt. "We started pretty high," said Gomez. "We were justified though. If it is more convenient for the state to spread the payments over a five- or 10-year period, then we want some kind of derived benefit for state employees."

According to PERS, if the payments as initially proposed were spread across 10 or 20 years, the principle and interest would have amounted to almost $4 billion. Over an extended amount of time, interest on a billion dollars compounds rather rapidly.

"We had our actuary provide a ceiling, and they had their actuary making sure what we were saying was real," said Gomez.

> In the end, we were very close, only about $300 million apart. The amount owed was a billion dollars, so the question was how much additional we could get in benefits for the accommodation of letting them have an interest rate payment. The unions were looking at the combination of getting a raise and some benefits at PERS. We weren't looking at it as a package. We were looking at it as fiduciaries and what is best for CalPERS. Once in a while our paths crossed, but not necessarily so.

"Cal PERS wanted much more than just the billion dollar settlement," said Pringle. They wanted three things. The first was a four percent cost of living adjustment (COLA) for their current retirees. That would have cost $700 million. The second was to allow second tier employees to move up to the first tier. In the first tier, an employee contributes five percent of their wage and the state contributes seven percent. If you made the first tier available to those currently in the second tier, the state would have had to pay the employee's five percent contribution to their own retirement, for the life of their contract. Otherwise, the unions would have complained that it was a pay cut. This would have cost the state $640 million. The final thing PERS wanted was to have the state pay for the five percent employee contribution for those already in the first tier for two years. This would have cost the state $760 million.

The court order demanded that any repayment agreement would be subject to additional financing charges. Not only would the state have to pay the $1.3 billion principle and $300 million for interest which was lost, but the state would also have to pay an 8¾ percent interest rate for any of the financing of the plans. When you do the math, it equals $293,836 in interest for every day the PERS payment is delayed.

The governor thought PERS was nowhere close to an acceptable agreement. PERS, on the other hand, believed it was possible to structure payment of the money owed so that the retirement system would be made whole as required by law, without creating devastating cuts to the state budget.

"The governor was off base in alleging that CalPERS was acting unreasonably by asking for comparable benefits in exchange for delayed payments over a 10-year period," said Gomez.

Wilson, argued Gomez, was essentially asking CalPERS to loan the state money at below market rates. This would violate both the California constitution and the federal tax laws. Under long-held principles of pension law, CalPERS would be allowed to accept delayed payments only as long as the beneficiaries were compensated by a comparable offsetting benefit.

"Maybe we would have gotten a little more in the long run, but it was all part of the negotiations," said Gomez. "We wanted full value plus one. Because of the court order we didn't have to consider anything less than full value, so we wanted to see how much we could get."

> We are a $120 billion business. A $30 million increase or a $50 million increase in the big scheme of things isn't really even significant. Now if you have a $1 billion debt and you get $1.1 billion by extending the payment, you've cut an ok deal but not a great one. It's all a percentage. It was a very interesting process and very close in the end. But this ain't horse shoes, and close doesn't count.

THE NEUTRON BOMB

During one of the Big 5 meetings, Senator Hurtt made a move to use the large budget surplus to repay the PERS debt.

> When I made the move to take the extra money and repay the PERS debt the room went silent. It's the fiscally responsible thing to do. We borrowed money, we should pay it back. The PERS people were

22

negotiating to use the court decision as leverage for a payback that would have netted them 3-4 times the original debt. Why should they get all that money? If we have a bill, and we have the money, then by gosh let's pay the bill and be done with it. Then by extension we don't have to fight about this other stuff because we don't have any money left.

The budget deadlock was dragging into its fifth week. As Pringle recalled, "Bustamante had a ton of pet projects. He had lists from every member of his caucus. It was very tough on him because he didn't have enough influence with his caucus to make a deal. He felt like he had to please everyone."

For a while, Governor Wilson was open to spreading the PERS repayment over as many as 10 years. This would have left room in the budget for a pay raise for state workers. What he wanted in return was a cut in the personal income tax.

Some Republicans perceived the move as having an additional bonus— driving a wedge between the unions. In this case, two of the largest unions wanted different outcomes. The California Teachers Association (CTA), arguably the most powerful force among the [lobbying groups], was adamantly opposed to a tax cut. The CTA viewed any tax cut as a threat to school funding. On the other side, the CSEA wanted the tax cut because the governor had tied any increase in state worker's wages to a middle-class tax cut.

Privately, some Republican lawmakers never believed that Wilson's personal income tax cut would ever fly in the legislature. Unable to convince members in his own party that the Democrats would ever swallow an income tax cut, Wilson, the tough ex-marine decided that he had to show them. Insiders believe that's why the income tax cut plan came at the last minute, in the middle of the Big 5 negotiations. Hurtt recalls,

> We had all those negotiations, and then pops the Wilson "tax cut," after we had already been talking for weeks. Once we finally got [welfare reform] taken care of, then the governor threw his "tax reduction" at us. The Dems were really antagonistic towards that idea. I was a little antagonistic myself. If you looked at it, it was actually a tax increase because it raised the brackets. The net effect would have been an increase in revenue by creating a more progressive tax towards the top end. I voiced my problem with that, and Wilson responded by saying that that was the only thing we could sell. I disagreed with that.

According to Kevin Sloat, the governor's deputy chief of staff, "Wilson made it very clear."[4] Either agree to the tax cut or he was going to pay back the PERS payment in one lump sum. The governor referred to it as a "Neutron Bomb," a weapon so powerful they decided not to build it. "Pete held all the cards on this one because the payment to the retirement system was the result of a court order. He didn't need the permission of the legislature to make the payment."

The Wilson administration had already produced a lengthy hit list of items to be sacrificed in case of a PERS repayment. This included money for state workers' raises, to forestall a raise in college fees, to speed up the death penalty appeals process, and to fund Wilson's own coastal initiative.

"In reality," said Sloat, "if the unions would have agreed to a tax cut it would have been a win-win. They may not have had all of their demands met, but a tax cut is just as good as a pay raise."

> We finally said okay let's talk about it. In our pre talks, our private talks, we said let's see where they stand on taxes. I opened the discussion and it didn't take long to see that they were dead set against it. The Republicans had a proposal, and [I asked the Democratic leadership] what don't you like about it. "We don't like anything about it" they said. In reality, it took about 30 minutes to decide that they didn't want to talk about any kind of tax reduction.

The decision was made by all to take the suggestions back to their caucuses. In the late evening the Big 5 met again, to report on what their caucus members had to say about the tax cut and the PERS repayment. "We all decided to take it back to our caucus in the afternoon. In the late evening, we were going to come back and report to each other. First about the [proposed] tax cut; but if there wasn't going to be a tax cut, then we would pay the bill," said Senator Hurtt. "Since the Democrats were dead set against the cut, we knew the outcome."

> We all came back the next day, and the governor was going to make the announcement. We walk in just before the press conference; the governor is on the phone with Lockyer. They were still negotiating a tax cut.

---

[4]Interview Kevin Sloat, Capitol 4081, February 11, 1998.

Lockyer made a few concessions but the money wasn't clean, so it never happened.

NOT OVER UNTIL . . . ?

Senator Hurtt disagreed with Pringle's proposed tax cut, but Pringle was still talking with Lockyer, and eventually they got an agreement to increase the dependent write off. It was after the fact. "I wasn't in favor because it wasn't going to start until the next year," said Hurtt. "It was a move to get whatever we could get. Well, the next year was supposed to be good as well, and we could have negotiated for a larger, better cut."

> The dependent credit was a good idea according to Pringle. Since California is not a zero budget state, one where the budget starts fresh each year, if the PERS repayment were made, there would be a large sum of money available in subsequent years. By implementing a dependent credit, the tax breaks would roll in and increase over a period of years.

> The dependent credit was to increase $50 per child in 1998, and an additional $100 in 1999. The total allowable amount would increase from $68 in 1997 to $218 in the year 2000. Since this is a credit, and not a deduction, the result is a dollar for dollar reduction in the actual amount owed. The fiscal impact would have been $95 million in 1998, $325 million in 1999, and $637 million in the year 2000.

"NO ONE" WINS AGAIN!

Hurtt was pushing for the personal income tax rate reduction, which would have affected everyone in the state. The dependent credit would only affect about 1/3 of the state. "I've gotten to the point where everyone wants their little piece," he said, "but there is no constituency for the total body politic. I think in terms of [what is] rational. They think in terms of what is politically marketable perception wise. I would never think the way they think. They don't like the way I think, because it won't align for them politically because they can't get what they want. Pringle wanted something to hang his hat on for his statewide race. His deal was the dependent credit.

"When we came back from the caucus meeting where we were discussing the tax cut and the repayment, they said, 'No tax cut.' Everyone knew the consequences; we were going to pay the bill. We never really agreed to it, it just happened. Common sense; cut and dried; pay the bill. Then we closed and we were finished."

Case 3

INTRODUCTION

The legal acceptability of acupuncture as an independent mode of treatment requiring specialized skills seemed politically premature at the time of this case. *Organized medicine,* largely represented by the California Medical Association, was steadfastly opposed: skin piercing was considered a form of surgery. If exotic forms of treatment gained a foothold, who could tell where it would end. Experimental procedures of dubious value should certainly be monitored and approved by a medical doctor. These arguments and others were not advanced casually. They represented the formal position of one of the most powerful lobbying organizations in California. So, why was it, *Time for the Underdog?* How did *Acupuncture Pierce the Status Quo?*

Note that while the CMA was powerful, it was under attack from other quarters, and some of its resources had to be diverted. Among its enemies were trial lawyers filing malpractice claims and collecting large judgments, and insurance-related entities seeking to create a favorable environment for health maintenance organizations (HMOs) so they could contain costs.

Notice the pre-existence of an organized community in San Francisco's Chinatown where acupuncture was practiced and accepted by large numbers or residents. Was the methodology with or without academic acceptance in the West? How might the attitudes of medical critics solidify some of its adherents? Would that solidification extend beyond practitioners, who might have thought they were being ridiculed culturally?

With respect to these and other questions, what was the impact of the media? Was the Reston article atypical of press reporting? Should it have been given the weight of scientific investigation? Does it matter whether it *should have?* Why did it have an extraordinary potential to influence?

Where did the legislative leaders, including Moscone, come from? Who were their constituents? Why might that have made a difference? From what point on the political spectrum do most San Francisco elected officials come? What personal attributes of Moscone might have made a difference?

What was the governor like? Why might that have made a difference? Why do you think Jerry Brown made his provocative comment about having signed the measure because of the financial influence of the supporters? The outcome, in its day, was far from anticipated. Yet, had someone handicapping the contest looked at matters mentioned, the odds against passage might have come down considerably.

A Time for the Underdog:
Acupuncture Pierces the Status Quo

Research and original writing by Senate Fellow Pablo Tagre

INTRODUCTION

Over a hundred acupuncturists and their guests gathered in a San Francisco Chinatown restaurant to attend the annual Chinese Medicine Day banquet.[1] There was a mood of festivity as performers entertained the attendees and caterers served an incredible variety of foods to the crowded auditorium-sized room. It was a night to celebrate the prosperity of Traditional Chinese Medicine (TCM) in California and the nation in general, as numerous presenters spoke at length of their profession's success and potential for growth. The evening was also an opportunity to remember their collective efforts; their long-fought struggle to win legitimacy in law and acceptance within the medical community.

Among the crowd were several people who played instrumental roles during the 1970s—a time when the legality and legitimacy of acupuncture was most intensely debated. The moderator reflected upon this time and recalled a bill that finally gave acupuncturists the authority to practice legally in the state of California. "Please, welcome our friend, a friend of the Chinese community, and the person who signed the law that made our profession legal—Governor Jerry Brown."

The audience broke into a long applause and cheered as the speaker walked leisurely toward the podium. He stood calmly on stage until the crowd subsided into complete silence. Then, in his cynical (because it wasn't true) brand of humor, and his nonconformist style, said, "well, I only signed

---

[1] The event took place on March 17, 2000, at the Meriwa Restaurant in San Francisco, with Dr. Robin Zhang the chief event coordinator.

the bill because you gave me a lot of money." In fact, while governor, Brown had maintained a serious interest in Asian cultural and religious practices.

THE PEOPLE'S CHAMPION

In 1974, Jerry Brown defeated a number of Democrat contenders for the party's gubernatorial bid. Among those contenders was George Moscone, a state senator from San Francisco. Moscone realized early in the race, however, that Brown would be the Democratic favorite, and therefore withdrew even before the identity of candidates became official. Though never close friends, Brown and Moscone's relationship was a collegial one. They maintained a good working relationship once Brown took office, and together passed several truly monumental pieces of legislation, including the nation's first gay rights bill, that would not have been possible under the Reagan administration.

That Moscone championed unconventional legislation is of little surprise to those who knew him. He is almost universally described as a devout advocate for the common person; the "unimportant"; those less able to speak for themselves. As mayor of San Francisco, he once presented the city's key to his barber. To those who protested, he smiled and simply said that a man had to look out for his barber. Perhaps the deeper meaning in this was that the working people play just as important a role in making the city great as those downtown in the financial district. Moscone loved *The City*.

He identified with the common person. He came from a family of modest means and had overcome a less-than-ideal childhood. Moscone's parents divorced when he was about eight years old, and his father was eventually institutionalized. His mother, Lena Moscone, raised her son alone and worked as a secretary during the week and as a liquor store clerk on weekends.

Moscone was admitted to the College of the Pacific (later University of the Pacific) on a basketball scholarship and thereafter attended Hastings Law School on an academic scholarship where he received his law degree in 1956. It was during this time that Moscone made acquaintances that would help shape his future career in public service; among them: John Burton,[2] brother of then Assemblymember Phillip Burton;[3] and Willie Brown,[4] also a student at Hastings and son of an African-American dirt farmer from Texas.

George Moscone first ran for a political post in an Assembly race. John Burton had recommended Moscone to his brother Phillip when a Democratic contender was needed to run in a heavily Republican district. Although he eventually lost the race, Moscone had done relatively well and therefore won enough gratitude from other Democratic party members to successfully run for a seat on the San Francisco Board of Supervisors in 1963. In 1966, he won a state senatorial bid, and only in his second year of office, was elected floor leader by his party.

The 1975 bill he carried on behalf of the acupuncturists would establish a procedure by which persons not licensed as physicians could be issued acupuncturist certificates, thereby allowing them to treat people upon a written referral by a physician. During the 1973-74 legislative session, a bill had been signed by then-Governor Ronald Reagan, which allowed acupuncture to be practiced on a limited basis in medical universities for research purposes. Nonphysician acupuncturists, however, were barred from practicing legally.

NOW, LET ME TELL YOU ABOUT MY APPENDECTOMY IN PEKING . . .

The push to pass legislation regarding acupuncture was relatively new. Acupuncture seemed to have jumped onto the political landscape out of nowhere. In fact, this practice only came to the general public's attention four years before the Moscone Bill, in 1971, when a well-respected reporter for the *New York Times* named James Reston wrote an article describing his experience in Peking with successful postappendectomy pain management using acupuncture needles.[5]

Reston had arrived in China a day before then-Secretary of State Henry Kissinger secretly flew there to meet with top ranking Chinese officials in

---

[2]Later to become state Senate president pro tem.
[3]Later to become a leading member of Congress.
[4]Later to become state Assembly Speaker; currently San Francisco mayor.
[5]*The New York Times*, July 26, 1971, 1, 6.

order to facilitate a visit by President Richard Nixon. A few days later Reston was hospitalized and treated for acute appendicitis. He writes:

> [The] hospital's surgical staff removed my appendix on July 17 after a normal injection of Xylocain and Benzocain, which anesthetized the middle of my body.
>
> There were no complications, nausea, or vomiting. I was conscious throughout, followed the instructions of Professor Wu as translated to me by Ma Yu-chen of the Chinese Foreign Ministry during the operation, and was back in my bedroom in the hospital in two and a half hours.
>
> However, I was in considerable discomfort if not pain during the second night after the operation, and Li Chang-yuan, doctor of acupuncture at the hospital, with my approval, inserted three long thin needles into the outer part of my right elbow and below my knees and manipulated them in order to stimulate the intestine and relieve the pressure and distension of the stomach.
>
> That sent ripples of pain racing through my limbs and, at least, had the effect of diverting my attention from the distress in my stomach. Meanwhile, Doctor Li lit two pieces of an herb called ai, which looked like the burning stumps of a broken cheap cigar, and held them close to my abdomen while occasionally twirling the needles into action.
>
> All this took about 20 minutes, during which I remember thinking that it was a rather complicated way to get rid of gas in the stomach, but there was noticeable relaxation of the pressure and distension within an hour and no recurrence of the problem thereafter.

President Nixon's subsequent visit to China in 1972 did much to further America's interest in Chinese traditions. This is not to say, however, that Reston's article was the first time America had ever heard of this procedure. Acupuncture has been practiced in North America since immigrants first came to this continent. However, among the English-speaking citizens of the United States, or at least the vast majority who had no daily contact with Asians, this article represents the first news of acupuncture to hit the mass English-speaking media.

Before this article appeared, acupuncture had been practiced only in urban Asian communities, discreetly and primarily by and for Asians. After this report the public at large increasingly embraced acupuncture.

FOLKLORE AND QUACKERY

Physicians, however, shunned the practice. Scientifically speaking, physicians thought the theories upon which Traditional Chinese Medicine (TCM) is based were highly questionable. The notion that two opposite forces in the body, called yin and yang, could be kept in balance by acupuncture so that Qi (the body's vital energy, pronounced "chee") could flow freely though the body, thereby promoting health and controlling disease, was considered absurd by most "mainstream" doctors.

Thus, acupuncture was believed by American doctors to be based on folklore and superstition. It had not been tested scientifically to their satisfaction, and could therefore not be considered a viable medical practice. Doctors also argued that if legitimized, the practice could pose a threat to the public's health. Patients would place unwarranted trust in acupuncturists, and ailments treatable by western medicine could go undiagnosed.

FUELING THE FLAMES

The public, however, demanded access to acupuncture treatment. And by 1974, it was legal for physicians, at least, to perform acupuncture. Chinese acupuncturists with years of experience, but who did not have an M.D., could be arrested for treating patients, and many were.

In July of 1973, Tomson Liang was ordered to appear in San Diego Superior Court on charges of practicing medicine without a license. Liang, the chief acupuncturist and director of Acupuncture and Herbs Research Inc. in Oceanside, California, was born in China and came to the United States in 1949. He said he started practicing the Chinese art of puncturing the body with needles to relieve pain when he was six years old, though he denied diagnosing or treating physical disorders.

In 1974, Miriam Lee who is today widely revered as the mother of acupuncture in California because of her heroic, pioneering efforts to legitimize acupuncture, also was arrested for practicing medicine without a license. This arrest added fuel to the fight to make a law that encompassed Traditional Chinese Medicine as it was practiced in China.

Ms. Lee had befriended another TCM advocate named Barbara Bernie. Suffering from chronic fatigue syndrome, Ms. Bernie sought treatment of acupuncturists. She was referred to an acupuncturist practicing surreptitiously in San Francisco. To avoid arrest, the acupuncturist, like others, practiced in a condemned Chinatown building. Ms. Bernie's meetings in a tiny room of a dilapidated building left a strong impression. She could not understand why a doctor who practiced a form of medicine legal in Europe for hundreds of years and respected in Asia for thousands of years would have to work under these conditions, or why she, as a patient, should have to break the law to receive the treatment she wished.

THE PUSH FOR LEGITIMIZATION

In 1971, Ms. Bernie began to fight the illegal status of acupuncture, making visits to the state's capitol to testify before committees. In 1972, she began the study of acupuncture at the Worsley School of Traditional Chinese Medicine in the United Kingdom. On a speaking tour with the school's head, she met the renowned acupuncturist Dr. Miriam Lee, who invited Ms. Bernie to study with her. Together the two lobbied in Sacramento urging the state legislature to pass legislation that would legalize acupuncture. Bernie and Lee befriended Senator George Moscone and worked with him to draft a bill that would allow the practice of acupuncture by nonphysicians.

Bernie and Lee wanted to pass a law that would permit the practice of acupuncture in much the same way as it existed in China. For them this meant that acupuncturists would have complete control over their patients, unrestrained and unsupervised by physicians.

Among the doctors' main concerns with such a proposition was the method that would be used to determine which individuals are qualified to perform acupuncture. Also of concern was the patient's quality of care. The California Medical Association (CMA) argued that treatment of ailments without consultation of a physician could endanger a patient's safety because it had not been proven that a practitioner of TCM could reliably detect harmful medical conditions such as cancer or a similar hard-to-diagnose condition.

If such legislation would pass, the CMA wanted to retain as much control over patients' treatment as possible. In response to CMA's concern, language was included in the bill stating that "acupuncture may not be performed by such a certified person without a prior diagnosis or referral of a physician and surgeon. . . ." CMA, however, managed in a subcommittee to change the "diagnosis or referral" provision to "diagnosis and referral," thereby giving doctors the power to allow a patient to consult an acupuncturist even after a diagnosis.

Senator Moscone objected to the change. In a letter to then-chair of the Assembly Health Committee Barry Keene,[6] Moscone wrote:

> I was quite cognizant of the fact that there was a demand that the bill should read "and" instead of "or." The reason I rejected this suggestion was that the problem had been fully solved by the diagnosis. Adding the additional requirement of a referral, since many M.D.s are strongly opposed to acupuncture, would place an unnecessary barrier between the patient and the acupuncturist.... I think in the interest of protecting the people of this state from being denied acupuncture, or submitting to the payment of tribute as a prerequisite to obtaining it, you should reappraise the question and amend the bill back to its original form.[7]

The CMA also suggested another solution, which would allow nonphysician acupuncturists to practice without endangering patient safety by establishing a procedure for both "licensing" and "certifying" acupuncturists. The bill would support a five-year period of certification during which the certified acupuncturist could practice under physician supervision. At the end of the five-year period, examinations for licensure would begin. Licensed acupuncturists could then practice independently.

The bill also included language to establish a procedure by which acupuncturists would be certified. A seven-member Acupuncture Advisory Committee would be appointed by the governor and regulated by the Board of Medical Examiners. The CMA agreed that a regulatory body must be created in order to regulate the profession, but they disagreed on the specified physical make-up of the committee. Instead of five acupuncturists and two physicians, the CMA strongly recommended, "an appropriate acupuncture board should be composed of four physicians (at least two of whom are experienced in acupuncture); one dentist acupuncturist; five nonphysician acupuncturists (to include Chinese, Japanese, and Korean members); a research scientist; and an academician." Some members of the CMA also objected to the governor's authority to make appointments, and recommended that the Board of Medical Examiners make the appointments.

---

[6]Later to hold the position of Senate Floor Leader, the position Moscone then held. The powerful Speaker of the Assembly, Leo T. McCarthy, was, like Moscone, a San Franciscan.

[7]Letter dated April 10, 1975.

The reference in the language to "and" instead of "or" was subsequently amended back to its original form, and the notion of a five-year supervision of "certified" acupuncturists by physicians was never seriously considered. The composition of the advisory committee as proposed by the CMA was likewise not adopted.

This bill (SB 86), like a similar bill (SB 2118) also carried George Moscone the year before passed all committee hearings and went to the governor for signature. The only difference between the two was that the earlier version went to the conservative Republican Governor Ronald Reagan, while SB 86 went to the desk of Jerry Brown where it was promptly signed into law.

LEGISLATION AFTER SB 86

Subsequent bills increased the degree to which acupuncturists could practice independent of western physicians. A 1978 bill, for example, eliminated the provision that required a patient to obtain "prior diagnosis or referral" by a medical doctor, dentist, podiatrist, or chiropractor before consulting an acupuncturist. In that same year, a bill was signed that authorized MediCal (i.e., California's version of federal Medicaid for the needy) payments for acupuncture. A 1980 bill expanded an acupuncturist's scope of practice to include electro-acupuncture, Oriental massage, and moxibustion, and authorized the prescribing of herbs for nutritional purposes by the practitioner. In 1984, a bill was passed that required health care service plans and nonprofit hospital service plans, that are not health maintenance organizations (HMOs) or self-insured plans to offer acupuncture coverage. Finally, in 1987, acupuncturists became legally included as "physicians" in the Workers' Compensation System for purposes of treating injured workers.

CONCLUSION

These legislative victories have granted acupuncturists the freedom to practice their profession in a manner that suggests acupuncture has gained approval and legitimacy. But what exactly "approval" and "legitimacy" mean in the case of acupuncture is unclear. The profession has undoubtedly gained legal approval and legitimacy, but Moscone's goal of legitimacy, as far as can be ascertained, meant to encompass much more. Moscone's legitimacy entailed not only legal recognition, but social and cultural acceptance as well. It can be argued, however, that acupuncture as a profession is viewed today in much the same way it was during the time Moscone and others advocated for its legitimization. Even as the popularity grows with the general public (an estimated 10 million treatments are given each year to more than one million American patients), most Western physicians and a large segment of the population, remain skeptical about the effectiveness of what they perceive as unproven and potentially dangerous folk remedies.

Did Moscone's SB 86, therefore, really *legitimize* the practice? Does legalization necessarily preclude legitimization? And if it is not a socially legitimate practice, what are the factors that keep it legally legitimate?

II.   Local Government, Community Action, and the Media

Case 4

INTRODUCTION

Even the most ardent free enterpriser—and Silicon Valley, part of the setting for *Room to Breathe*, is loaded with them—would concede that the marketplace is not the best arena for solving all of society's ills. An unregulated economy can even cause or exacerbate some problems. The extraordinary economic success of Silicon Valley drove property values so high that development pressures spread into areas once regarded as permanent open space. Some government intervention seemed necessary to virtually everyone. But how much; what kind; and with what powers?

Poor roads between Silicon Valley and the urban areas surrounding San Francisco Bay were something of a deterrent to sprawl. Farmers, whose income and lifestyle helped thwart development, hold most of the threatened land. Yet, are they all immune from the lure of sudden and fabulous wealth should their land be developable? When a state agency set up to protect open space is called in, there is massive resistance to the possibility that their land or development rights will be acquired against their will, despite a constitutional guarantee of compensation at fair market value. But what is fair market value? Is it calculated on the assumption that the land is developable, or on the assumption that development will never be allowed?

Two levels of division are evident: The divide that exists between Valley residents who favor development (at least for themselves) and those who want to maximize coastal open space; and the divide between farmers and residents of coastal communities over exercise of the government's power of eminent domain.

The case demonstrates many of the complexities involved in government decision making. Yet, you can be sure that at any public debate, someone will jump up and ask simplistically why her opponent is against the preservation of open space. Notice, the influence of *cultural* assumptions about government (e.g., the taking of property is tyranny); the inertia caused by ambivalent *motives* (e.g., should we fix the roads?); the skewed impacts that occur with different rules about how voting outcomes occur (e.g., supermajorities; population versus acreage); and the special interest influence of money on elections (even when the objective of the major donor is not clear).

It is hard to not sympathize with the apparent underdog in the episode involving the Russian Orthodox nuns. And yet, was the order not just another developer as far as the potential for a large and adverse impact on open space? Was MSROD to stand idly by and let it happen notwithstanding their official responsibilities? Given the advantage of "Monday morning quarterbacking," how would you have handled it? Or, was the outcome was inevitable?

Special Districts: Room to Breathe—The Midpeninsula Regional Open Space District

Research and original writing by Senate Fellow Megan Wong

OPEN SPACE

The San Francisco Bay Area continues to grow dramatically despite worsening traffic congestion, exorbitant living costs, periodic seismic intrusions, and geographic limitations. At the same time, it's unique blend of culture, climate, and economic opportunity is internationally recognized. One of its great attractions is easy access to the wonders of nature. Anyone willing to drive a few hours in any direction can find snow-capped mountains, redwood forests, ocean beaches, wild rivers, and, closer in, woods, lakes, parks, and miles of scenic trails.

The Peninsula, upon whose northern tip sits *The City*—San Francisco of course—boasts a unique combination of cultural and economic assets including Stanford University and Silicon Valley. Those features are complemented by a rich abundance of open space preserves and hiking and riding trails that afford access to the area's natural beauty.

One of the most magnificent parts of California, perhaps of the entire U.S., is the breathtakingly picturesque coastal road known as Highway 1. Clinging precariously to the rocky slopes overlooking the Pacific Ocean, it snakes steadily up the Pacific Coast to northern Mendocino County where it joins Highway 101 and continues into Oregon.

A large and sometimes rugged segment of this highway runs through the San Francisco Bay Area. On the part of the coast within San Mateo County, the midpeninsula, Highway 1 is the main artery. From the bay (or eastern) side of San Mateo County, one gets to it by traveling west on Highway 92, crossing a small, mountainous ridge, and arriving at the coastal city of Half Moon Bay.

Along the southern part of the San Mateo County coast, Peninsula residents treasure some of the most unspoiled and agriculturally productive open space anywhere. Fields of flowers, artichokes, Brussels sprouts, and pumpkins adorn miles of gentle hills and rolling plains that spill westward to the Pacific Ocean. Visitors and Bay Area residents use the coastal beaches and trails with little regard to season or weather conditions.

BEFORE IT'S ALL GONE

Recently, people in the more urbanized section of the coast, residents of Montara, Moss Beach, El Granada, and Half Moon Bay, have begun to feel pressured by development. In the spring of 1997, a local environmental group known as FOCOS (Friends of Coastal Open Space) petitioned local city agencies and councils to address the problem of diminishing open space in coastal San Mateo County. The officials concurred and asked the Midpeninsula Regional Open Space District (MROSD) to formally investigate and recommend a plan to protect the coast.

MROSD was created in 1972. Approved by a ballot measure introduced by a group of conservationists in Santa Clara County, its mission is "To create a greenbelt of open space lands, linking district preserves with other public parklands,"[1] in order to preserve the natural scenic beauty of the midpeninsula for generations to come. Four years after its inception, the district annexed land in southwest San Mateo County and, not long after that, added a small portion of Santa Cruz County. By MROSD definition, open space is land or water in its natural state, used for agriculture, or essentially undeveloped. Its basic policy says, "In short, open space means *room to breathe.*"

Today, MROSD owns and manages almost 46,000 acres of open space in the area between San Francisco Bay and the crest of the Santa Cruz Mountains in 24 open space preserves ranging in size from 55 to over 12,000 acres.

---

[1]MROSD website—http://www.openspace.org

SPECIAL DISTRICTS

Special districts are a form of local government that deliver specific public services to a community or region. They are not state agencies, city or county governments, school districts, or redevelopment agencies, but they are governed by state law. There are thousands of special districts in California ranging in scope from basic fire protection and water districts to sewage treatment, mosquito abatement, cemetery, and open space districts. Special districts are formed when residents or landowners want new or higher levels of services. The unique advantage of special districts is that they localize both the costs and benefits of public services. You know what you pay for and see what you get.

Special districts have the power to enter into contracts, employ workers, tax, levy assessments, and acquire property either through purchase from willing sellers or, in some cases, eminent domain. Although they have corporate powers (i.e., the ability to construct public works, deliver services, raise money, etc.), special districts do not possess police power (i.e., the direct ability to regulate behavior).

Like most special districts, an elected seven-member board of directors makes policy decisions and effectively administers the MROSD. While primarily concerned with habitat protection and preserving the natural environment, some development is usually allowed for public access, low-intensity recreation, trails and related facilities. However, their actual provision falls on the cities and counties according to MROSD's basic policy. Currently, the MROSD manages several open space preserves on the Peninsula. Residents who live within the district's boundaries pay a small portion of their property tax in order to fund the activities of the district—acquisition administration, management, maintenance, and over-sight.

"LIKE, THERE ARE SO MANY PEOPLE IN THE VALLEY"

Conservationists sought an open space district on the Peninsula to deal with development pressure from Silicon Valley in the late 1960s. Then came the Internet explosion, resulting in phenomenal growth in population and wealth throughout the Peninsula and South Bay. It spawned an unprece-dented increase in property values that impacted the coast of San Mateo. Although the midpeninsula was the vortex, development pressures reached fever pitch throughout the Bay Area. To some, the threat seemed clear and certain: "High-tech" professionals accumulating wealth would look increasingly toward the pastoral hills of the coast—sufficiently far from the rat race of San Jose and Santa Clara to feel "away from it all," yet close enough to Silicon Valley to commute to work without too much hassle.[2] The best of both worlds for affluent professionals.

˙ GOING THROUGH THE PROPER CHANNELS

In the spring of 1997, three representative bodies and a grassroots preservation organization (the Half Moon Bay City Council, the Pescadero Municipal Advisory Council, the Mid-Coast Community Council and the Coastal Alliance) urged MROSD to consider coastal protection options. Three of the four organizations draw most of their membership from residents *north* of Half Moon Bay. Only PMAC's membership is composed solely of residents from *south* of it.

The alternatives identified by MROSD included involving an existing public agency (e.g., county, state, or federal park departments), forming a new special district, involving the state Coastal Conservancy or the Coastal Commission, and annexing the San Mateo County coast area.

After extensive investigation and review, meetings with stakeholders, and deliberation and debate, including two public meetings, the MROSD board concluded that annexing the area into the existing district would be the most effective way to proceed. To gauge public reaction, the board put advisory Measure F on the November ballot: "In order to preserve open space resources on the San Mateo County Coast, shall the Midpeninsula Regional Open Space District extend its boundary west of Skyline to the San Mateo County Coast, from the southern boundary of Pacifica to the Santa Cruz County line?" Only communities affected were allowed to vote on the measure. It passed, 55 percent to 45 percent.

Although it passed with an absolute majority, the breakdown of votes reveals another story. When the votes on Measure F are separated geographically, a telling pattern emerges: urban north coast residents from Montara, Moss Beach, El Granada, Princeton, Miramar and (a more closely divided)

---

[2]Landowner Michael Murphy disagreed, saying "the commute is notoriously terrible." Letter to the case editor, June 6, 2000.

Half Moon Bay overwhelmingly approved the expansion of MROSD; a majority of residents of the more rural south coast voted against it. The rural residents who own most of the land in question claimed they were outvoted because there are roughly 25,000-30,000 voters in north coast cities and roughly 10,000 south of Half Moon Bay.

The vocal southern landowning minority did not believe the end result of expansion for them would be room to breathe. It would mean, they feared, cultural and economic extinction in the coils of eminent domain.

EMINENT DOMAIN: IMMINENT CONTROVERSY

Eminent domain is the inherent power of government to take private land for public use, provided there is a finding of public necessity and fair market value is paid. Eminent domain can be invoked when a government agency needs to install underground pipes through a person's backyard or expand a highway over someone's land. These actions are typically viewed as necessary and prudent uses of governmental power; inconveniencing a few for the benefit of many.

Understandably, it is one of the most controversial of governmental powers, and many feel that the government has abused the power far too often. For example, many dislocations occur in low-income areas, or so it is alleged, where property values are lower and people are less able to afford litigation.

According to MROSD General Manager Craig Britton, government will usually not invoke the power unless it sees no other way. His view, which contrasts with that of critics, is that a property owner routinely "gets a great deal" during an eminent domain proceeding. The owner can negotiate knowing a favorably high price is legally guaranteed, and the public agency wants to avoid litigation expenses and delay. Many cases, he says, are handled by attorneys on a contingency fee basis with no expense to the owner, until and unless recovery occurs. Also, jurors more often identify with property owners than with government agencies, increasing the possibility of awards favorable to the owner. In response to criticism, the government has included relocation requirements, mediation mandates, and provisions prohibiting deflated pricing. Nevertheless, that government can legally override property rights makes people nervous, especially those who have little trust in government.

A DIFFERENT KIND OF PLACE

The communities west of Skyline Boulevard (Hwy 35) consider themselves unique and poorly understood or appreciated by outsiders, including "baysiders." There is greater involvement in community issues, especially development matters. Citizens delight in showing up at city council meetings, especially when contentious issues are to be decided. But not all "coastsiders" think alike. Thus, when MROSD proposed expanding its boundaries west of Skyline Boulevard from the southern border of Pacifica to the northern border of Santa Cruz County, people from diverse community groups armed for battle, prepared to struggle over longstanding intracoastal divisions and distrust.

WHY DO THEY NEED EMINENT DOMAIN?

Opponents disagreed that district expansion via eminent domain was the only solution. They pointed to alternatives such as conservation easements—buying the "conservation rights" as the Sonoma County Agricultural Preservation and Open Space District, and the Peninsula Open Space Trust (POST), had done.

Critics of eminent domain, like farmers Stan Pastorino and Jack Olsen, and wealthy south coast landowner Michael Murphy, point to the existing development restrictions outlined in the Local Coastal Plan (LCP) for the rural area south of Half Moon Bay. Depending on to whom one speaks, under the current LCP, a landowner (unless a smaller parcel was "grandfathered" in) must own between 40 and 160 acres—depending on how hilly they are—for the right to build one house on land in the south coast. In addition, there are restrictions regarding setbacks (the siting of a development in relation to the landscape), scenic corridors (development is restricted in designated areas), and use of prime agricultural land. Olsen and other opponents of eminent domain mentioned that in the years since World War II, population growth on the south coast has been incredibly slow. For 50-60 years, there has been very little development, even less than what the LCP would otherwise have allowed. According to Olsen, only nine new homes have been built since 1980. To opponents of eminent domain these statistics prove there is no need for additional safeguards to protect the south coast from development. Letting the district come to the coast with the power of eminent domain would infringe on their rights as landowners.

KEEP BIG GOVERNMENT OFF OUR LAND

South coast landowners, farmers, and rural interests feel threatened by what they view as the ever-increasing presence and power of the government. According to Eric Rice, a Half Moon Bay resident and local reporter who covered the expansion controversy for the *Half Moon Bay Review*, "The south coast area has a different ethos; it's more individualistic, not wanting government intervention . . . people chose to live there because it was more rural."[3] Zoe Kersteen-Tucker, a local environmental advocate from Moss Beach, said, "Any form of additional government is viewed as undesirable."[4] Many opponents of the MROSD expansion have lived on the south coast for at least a generation, often two, three, or even four. Peter Marchi, a Pescadero farmer, summed it up nicely: "We are basically country people, and we work together on our own and with ourselves. Bringing in the other agency would change the way we have done things for hundreds of years."[5] At Coastal Advisory Committee (CAC) meetings, many residents said they felt threatened by the prospect of losing more than property; they feared losing their family history and their way of life.

LINES DRAWN IN THE COASTAL SAND

The battle lines between agricultural and environmental interests were drawn long before MROSD arrived. San Mateo County Supervisor Rich Gordon connected the current contention over MROSD expansion to past environmental versus agricultural debates: "There is a history of conflict between the environmental community and the agricultural community. . . people are already not liking each other and are pretty suspicious of each other." Kersteen-Tucker said the property rights interests blamed the environmental interests for implementing the Local Coastal Plan that regulates land use on the coast. She said that many people south of Half Moon Bay regard environmentalists with suspicion, viewing them as something like "educated yuppies that move over here and want to take

---

[3]Telephone interview, March 1, 2000.
[4]Telephone interview, March 9, 2000.
[5]Deirdre Pettit, *Half Moon Bay Review*, November 21, 1999.

over."[6] In fact, the two parties are often on opposite sides of the table when negotiating such things as water issues or determining agricultural best management practices. Kersteen-Tucker felt that because environmentalists were instrumental in passing the Local Coastal Plan (which is extremely restrictive of development), south coast landowners distrusted them in general. Underlying suspicion on both sides contributed greatly to the intractable nature of the debate over expansion of MROSD.

Because it was obvious that MROSD's expansion was going to be contentious, the district convened a 13-member Coastal Advisory Committee (CAC). Its purpose was to review district policies in light of the specific needs and desires of the coastal community and to make recommendations relating to land acquisition, agricultural use, and eminent domain. Possibly to pacify objecting rural residents, membership was deliberately made as inclusive as possible—the Pescadero Municipal Advisory Council, the Half Moon Bay City Council, the Midcoast Community Council, the San Mateo Board of Supervisors, the San Mateo Farm Bureau, POST, the San Mateo County Agricultural Commission, and the Cabrillo Unified School District. Three members of the MROSD board of directors' ad hoc committee were added, raising the number to 11 members who would then select three at-large members to round out community representation at 14. CAC Chair Supervisor Rich Gordon noted that, "In bringing together a Coastal Advisory Committee, the board . . . sought to identify people who represented the divergent perspectives . . . 50 percent of the people who supported annexation and 50 percent who opposed it."[7]

STONEWALLING DEBATE

Eminent domain quickly rose to the top of the agenda. Rich Gordon's recollection was that some members effectively stonewalled the discussions until the issue of eminent domain was settled to their satisfaction: "What you essentially ended up with was a group that was going to have a difficult, if not impossible, time ever coming to a recommendation that a majority could agree upon. . . . [T]he agricultural community said that . . . until [eminent domain] was addressed, they weren't going to discuss anything else.

---

[6]Telephone interview, March 9, 2000.
[7]Telephone interview, March 16, 2000.

[T]he other side couldn't move them. After nine months of debate and discussion, it became clear that unless you dealt with eminent domain, you couldn't do anything."[8]

CAC member-at-large Chris Thollaug said: "When people just shut down discussion . . . you have to step back from the content . . . and deal with the process. . . . [W]hen the folks . . . supposed to make a decision shut down that process, . . . the public interest isn't served."[9]

MROSD eventually realized that it was politically necessary to bring the opponents of eminent domain on board. Rich Gordon said, "In order to get a tax to support the activities of annexation, they were going to need a two-thirds vote. So, . . . pragmatically, you had to get some of the folks who voted 'no' to annexation to vote 'yes' to taxation. And the only way you would accomplish that would be if you really did something to address their concerns about eminent domain."[10]

COME DANCE, BUT DON'T HOG THE FLOOR

Enter Stan Pastorino, a local flower grower, longtime resident of Half Moon Bay, and Farm Bureau representative on the CAC. According to Pastorino, the farming community did not want MROSD on the coast at all. When its expansion seemed inevitable, some south coast landowners decided to make annexation more palatable. Pastorino, fellow CAC member Neil Curry, and south coast resident Bill Cook circulated a petition among south coast landowners that said they would support district efforts to annex south coast land (and an inevitable tax increase) if, and only if, the board agreed to give up the power of eminent domain. They gathered 250 signatures; but those few signatures represented 20,000-30,000 acres of south coast land.

Not everyone was thrilled. Pescadero farmer Peter Marchi had mixed feelings: "It's like paying somebody not to be able to take from you." In the end, he signed: "By inviting them with a compromise we asked them to come

---

[8]Telephone interview, March 16, 2000.
[9]Telephone interview, March 15, 2000.
[10]Telephone interview, March 16, 2000.

with a few guidelines: When you come to our home you can't steal our home."[11]

Said Kersteen-Tucker,

> We have to enact regulations and protections that cover us not just right now, not just two years from now, not just five years from now but 50 years from now. They'll tell you, "why do we need them [the MROSD]? We already have extraordinarily restrictive land-use regulations in the coastal zone"—which we do. But, you have to remember that we're sitting less than 30 miles away from one of the largest economic engines on earth, namely the Silicon Valley. So, the pressure to erode those strict land-use regulations is intense; and it's increasing with every passing day.[12]

Kersteen-Tucker felt that eminent domain was essential should development pressure ever get out of control: "It puts an additional set of teeth into the already strict land-use regulations."[13]

ALMOST A RELIGION

Supervisor Rich Gordon recalled the unique character of the controversy over eminent domain: "I began to feel that this was a religion . . . a belief system."[14] With one or two exceptions, members of the 13-person CAC all supported the concept of maintaining open space and agricultural land. It became clear they were not discussing different goals, there was simply great disagreement on the means. With some frustration and a hint of irony, Gordon noted, "Usually, if people agree upon where you want to get to, you'll find a way to get there. In this situation, the positions were so [entrenched] that we could not. . . . For the ag community, the land is both the place they live and the way they make their money. So, any threat to the land is perceived . . . as a threat both to their home and to their livelihood."[15]

---

[11]Deirdre Pettit, Half Moon Bay Review, November 21, 1999.
[12]Telephone interview, March 9, 2000.
[13]Telephone interview, March 9, 2000.
[14]Telephone interview, March 16, 2000.
[15]Telephone interview, March 15, 2000.

Painful memories of past experiences influenced the debate. One was the proposed expansion of the Golden Gate National Recreation Area (GGNRA) to the Santa Cruz County line in the late 1960s. Congressman Phil Burton and members of the California Legislature, including his brother John Burton, spearheaded the effort. Landowners fought long and hard to keep the GGNRA off their land. One sixth-generation resident of the Santa Cruz Mountains recalled his family's experience. A parks agency of the state or federal government purchased a portion of his family's forest after eminent domain proceedings in order to include it in the GGNRA. Now, he said, people are allowed to hike, bike, and ride on his property if they have the necessary permit. He came to the CAC meeting to warn that the threat of eminent domain was very serious and real. Another speaker told about losing a pasture to eminent domain during the construction of a highway. Said MROSD General Manager Craig Britton, "They have a collective memory that goes back quite a ways."[16]

BULLYING RUSSIAN NUNS

Another event that escalated sensitivity to eminent domain involved a group of Russian Orthodox nuns seeking a religious center and convent. Within MROSD jurisdiction near a narrow highway that runs along the top of Skyline Ridge, the center would have generated incompatible development and increased visitor traffic. According to MROSD's Craig Britton, the church property separated vital open space from housing areas further south, constituted a significant wildlife corridor, and was adjacent to a state-designated scenic highway and the Bay Area Ridge Trail system. Britton had contacted the Catholic Church 20 years prior about the possibility of acquiring the land, but was told the district had nothing to worry about; the land was open space and would remain so. If that changed, MROSD would be informed that the property was up for sale.

In the spring of 1998, the Catholic Church decided to sell the land to the Russian Orthodox nuns rather than to MROSD. Desperate, the district's board of directors resolved to preserve the valuable parcel of open space the only way that they could—invoking the power of eminent domain. MSROD came off looking like a bully. Religious and civic groups rallied to the nuns'

---

[16]Telephone interview, March 7, 2000.

defense. In the amazing public spectacle that ensued, which eventually became an international incident, the nuns won.

San Jose Mercury News reporter Marilee Enge saw the controversy as a brilliant public relations move by the nuns. She recalled a group of nuns, in full habit, filing into an official public meeting and rousing public outrage. While the nuns finally agreed to scale back their original development plans, MSROD backed down.

Reflecting on the unexpected controversy, Britton said, "I would . . . still have [had] to recommend that we go forward [with acquiring the property through eminent domain] because the property was so important as public open space. But maybe if that [had been] tempered with my knowledge of the political fallout, I might not have."[17]

When MROSD's proposed expansion to the San Mateo County Coast came up for debate, the incident remained a flashpoint of passion and controversy over eminent domain.

A SUDDEN INFUSION OF FUNDS

Into this hypersensitive context stepped Michael Murphy, a local high-tech businessperson and farmer. Not a traditional row-crop farmer himself, Murphy says he believes in high-intensity, high-value crops that can generate revenues sufficient to keep farmers in business.

Chris Thollaug, one of the three at-large members of the CAC, observed that Murphy's vision of agriculture was more related to tourism than agriculture, a boutique operation with a bed and breakfast, a gift shop, and maybe some llamas.

Nonetheless, Murphy found he had as much at stake in stopping the expansion of the MROSD as conventional south coast farmers and added his abundant financial resources to the fight against expansion. His ostensible concern was the uncertainty of future district policies. "What about in 40 years, when my walnut trees mature?" asked Murphy.[18] He had an idyllic vision of the future of his land, which, in addition to his existing home, might include new dwellings where his two grown children and their families could one day reside. Above all, Murphy, like other south coast landowners, did

---

[17]Telephone interview, March 7, 2000.
[18]Telephone interview, April 20, 2000.

not trust his future to the hands of an entity that lacked coastal representation but had the power of eminent domain.

Murphy spent $54,000 of his own money to defeat Measure F. The infusion of funds made the debate more prominent in the media, although it is unclear whether it accomplished much else. Several individuals referred to Murphy's campaign as fear mongering designed to stir up the emotions of south coast landowners.

Chris Thollaug said Murphy used scare tactics to rally opposition. He cited a political mailing containing a picture of a single-family dwelling backing up to some woods. The text implied that the person's home—any person's home—was in danger of being taken away in favor of "open space." Murphy said the inference was correct.[19]

Kersteen-Tucker said Murphy had a development plan for his ranch south of Half Moon Bay; but the Local Coast Plan—the plan that dictates land development policies and restrictions—was designed to preserve traditional open-field crops, not more intensive uses. Thollaug believed that Murphy feared a restriction on increased density credits on his south coast ranch because he planned to one day develop his land in a manner incompatible with open space preservation. Murphy objected saying there is no evidence he intends houses or anything other than high value crops.[20]

Local environmental activist Kersteen-Tucker saw parallels between the controversy and agriculture vs. environmental debates across the country—loggers in the Pacific Northwest, farmers in the Central Valley, ranchers in Wyoming wanting to protect their livelihood and way of life against so-called "preservationists." Most interviewees agreed that this debate is not unique to the San Mateo County coast.

Wherever there is undeveloped land, there is often a contingent with long roots in the area, perceiving its economic activities and lifestyle as a bastion against urbanization. Landowners believe they have been good stewards of the land and the government should stay out of their business.

Environmentalists, originating in urban or suburban areas that were unable to prevent their own degradation, are concerned that without the proper legal protections, their experience will be repeated and additional open space will be lost.

---

[19]*Letter* to the case editor, June 6, 2000.
[20]*Letter* to the case editor, June 6, 2000.

As Kersteen-Tucker reflected, "There's probably a lot more common ground than we think and it just takes, unfortunately, a few mistakes made to lose a whole lot of ground."[21]

WE GIVE UP!

In November of 1999, 18 months after MROSD initially considered annexing the San Mateo County coast by whatever means necessary, it surrendered its power of eminent domain in the coastal annexation area—or seemed to have. Board members recognized they needed to overcome both the stonewalling and the inevitable difficulty of obtaining the two-thirds vote needed to pass the taxation measure to fund annexation-related activities. As Kersteen-Tucker put it, "The district decided, wisely, that there was more to be gained by being over here without eminent domain than continuing to fight for eminent domain."[22]

The controversy is far from finished. San Mateo County Farm Bureau Executive Director Jack Olsen and eminent domain opponent Michael Murphy both believe that one of the largest remaining obstacles to MROSD expansion is the issue of funding—whether or not a tax increase to fund the district's activities in the proposed annexation area will be approved by the necessary two-thirds. But as they pledged when they signed the petition, because the district gave up the threat of eminent domain, they will put their support behind efforts to bring the district to the coast, rallying community and financial support in any way they can.

Having settled the issue of eminent domain, the district began the formal application process to the two LAFCOs—San Mateo and Santa Clara—that must approve the district's proposed expansion. The district must still decide how it will officially and legally assure relinquishment of its eminent domain power. Some believe it can be written into the LAFCO application; others think it involves changing state law. There seems no end to the uncertainty. Including whether there will be room to breathe.

---

[21]Telephone interview, March 9, 2000.
[22]Telephone interview, March 9, 2000.

Case 5

INTRODUCTION

When the Northridge earthquake severely damaged Los Angeles' key arterial, the Santa Monica Freeway connecting the city with the San Fernando Valley (not to mention southern California with points north), it was repaired in a matter of weeks. The decision to repair it in the shortest possible time—miraculously short as it turned out—was made largely by the mayor and state transportation authorities. In *Shake, Rattle, and Push*, it took a decade to repair the damage northern California's Loma Prieta earthquake did when a Cypress Freeway overpass collapsed causing numerous deaths and injuries. The delay resulted largely from the question of whether to simply repair it with seismic improvements or relocate it.

The Cypress had never been regarded as a benefit to the small and politically powerless West Oakland community where it was built. Look for evidence of this in the case; it was really built to serve the interests of others who had to drive through the area. It was also a symbol of the times. Freeways were an icon of the future of transportation and a mainstay of growth then thought desirable in every way. That it severed a community with a history and a culture of note reminds us of the second-class status of African Americans, especially, but not exclusively, those who are poor. It reminds us of the power of the automobile, construction, and oil interests clustered and reflected in a state agency called Caltrans. Today, the decision to build the Cypress would have been reached by a very different route. The earthquake presented an opportunity to remake the decision under contemporary standards. Outsiders still needed the freeway link. Caltrans still had its responsibility. But this time it was West Oaklanders who were determined to decide where *their* freeway would be built!

Follow with care the decision-making process, noting that this time, contrasted with the first time and with the Santa Monica repairs described above, the process was inclusive and collective. The demands of the community were considerable. The status of African Americans and their leadership had changed. Moreover, the efforts to secure a decision involved the additional components of compensation and remediation for harm the

57

original Cypress had inflicted on West Oakland. Thus, both the process—allowing everyone in and bringing them together—and the substance—finding a new and suitable location and including compensatory amenities—caused a decade-long delay. Were all or most of the expectations met? Given the delay, how in the world could the West Oakland community possibly be considered a winner?

The real questions: How much weight should be given to the argument that *the decision process itself*, the realization of collective empowerment, however long it took, had a positive value that cannot be overestimated? And how much weight should be given to the *community consciousness* of West Oakland that it will never again allow itself to be divided for the benefit of others, no matter how powerful—not business interests, not railroads, not state highway departments, and not even those holding the federal purse strings?

Shake, Rattle, and Push:
West Oakland Moves a Freeway

Original research and writing by Senate Fellow Parissh Anthony Knox

WEST OAKLAND

Cypress is a textbook example of new transportation realities in
California and elsewhere . . . neighborhoods are no longer willing to be
sacrificed to the transportation gods.
— *Sacramento Bee* July 25, 1997

Loma Prieta's biggest effect on transportation would be felt over the next
10 years as Caltrans undertook the world's largest seismic retrofitting
program. . . . Billions of state transportation dollars—not to mention
attention and urgency—that would have been directed to highway and
transit improvements to relieve congestion and maintain the state's
highway system was instead redirected to seismic retrofitting.
— *San Francisco Chronicle October* 16, 1999

ONLY A STONE'S THROW

In the shadows of the nearby Port of Oakland and the old Oakland Army
Base sits one of the oldest neighborhoods in the East Bay. Urban industrial
West Oakland is enmeshed in a complex web of freeways and interchanges—
I-80, 580, 880, and 980. It is a common sight to commuters on the Bay Area
Rapid Transit System and drivers on the new Cypress Freeway. But despite
its easy accessibility from most points in the bay area, West Oakland has
long been an isolated community.

Recently, however, the economic engines of Media Gulch and Silicon
Valley have been revving up in the East Bay. The growth and investment
they have spun off are evident throughout the community. Yet, West
Oakland remains one of the city's most distressed neighborhoods. It is home

to more than its share of diesel truck traffic, noise, environmental contamination, crime, and poverty. Nearly 75 percent of the population is African American; many of them living in poverty. West Oakland's proximity to San Francisco and the area's inexpensive property are beginning to attract newcomers, causing longtime residents to worry that they will be squeezed out by gentrification.

Emeryville, West Oakland's neighbor to the north, has become a booming commercial success with an abundance of big new retail stores, lofts, and hotels. To the south, Fremont was recently rated one of the most livable cities in America. And Oakland Mayor Jerry Brown has grabbed headlines with his campaign to bring 10,000 new residents to downtown Oakland and his efforts to make Jack London Square a regional destination. Change and renewal is happening all over Oakland, and some of it is starting to spill over into West Oakland. For many, the sound of renewal began with the fearsome rumble that rippled from the Loma Prieta fault and sent the Cypress Freeway crashing down in a deafening—and deadly—roar.

JOBS, MIGRANTS, AND CHANGE

West Oakland sits at the western terminus of a vast railroad system that, over the years, has included the Union Pacific, the Southern Pacific, and the Santa Fe. Traffic was a constant. Whether by passenger car, freight train, or on foot; people were on the go. Ferries, once supplanted by "The Great Bridge Across the Bay," are lately making a comeback.

Prior to War World II, West Oakland was a community of proud families, Victorian homes, and neighborhood churches. Seventh Street, the heart of this vibrant community, was lined with restaurants, hair salons, barber shops, nightclubs, cafes, and retail stores bustling with activity. Legendary musicians like Louis Armstrong performed at local jazz clubs. West Oakland was a cultural Mecca in the East Bay, a racially mixed community where people could find work no matter what their color.[1]

The 1950s brought renewal—manufacturing jobs were springing up everywhere. Bay Area military bases and shipyards drew black people from

---

[1]Ron Dellums and H. Lee Halterman, *Lying Down With the Lions: A Public Life from the Streets of Oakland to the Halls of Power* (Boston: Beacon Press, 2000).

throughout the nation to the West Coast, most of them from the South. As Congressman Ron Dellums wrote: "West Oakland would be the port of entry for blacks in northern California, just as San Jose was for immigrants from Mexico or San Francisco for Asians. Most of the black migrants would disembark the train at Sixteenth and Wood Streets in West Oakland and settle within blocks of the industrial base that had lured them west in the first place."[2]

Long before the term NIMBY, (not-in-my-backyard), communities had to struggle with the impact of other people's decisions, and West Oakland was no exception. At the time the original Cypress Freeway was built, West Oakland was a community with little political influence.

Although people working at the bases and shipyards earned good money, housing segregation in the 1940s kept black folks bottled up. West Oakland was home to a large segment of the Bay Area African-American community. "Over the years," wrote Ron Dellums in his memoir, *Lying Down With Lions*,

> West Oakland lost its integrated character—certainly its white majority—becoming more and more black, finally almost exclusively so. New black migrants filled the houses of the departing white ethnics, who were moving to neighborhoods in the northern and eastern parts of the city, or out of Oakland altogether, presaging the "urban flight" that would begin in earnest in the 1950s.

As the population shifted, light industry located in West Oakland, significantly impacting the surrounding neighborhoods. Businesses built factories next to residential homes and automobile dismantling shops next to recreational parks. Critics complained that these resources were designed to help the suburban communities around Oakland, with benefits to West Oakland an afterthought.

A COMMUNITY DIVIDED

Of all the developments affecting West Oakland, the double-decker Cypress Freeway topped the list. The viaduct literally split the community. Stretching 1.5 miles, the freeway was the biggest neighbor on the block. By

---

[2]*Ibid.*

the time the Cypress was complete, rows of homes had been bulldozed and hundreds of families displaced.

The Cypress Viaduct, built in the late 1950s, was part of the Nimitz Freeway that runs down the east side of San Francisco Bay from Oakland to San Jose. For some, in those days when the automobile was king, it was a remarkable achievement and a real asset. For others, even then, the huge structure was a frightening eyesore. "It was the glamour girl of freeways in an era when they were still synonymous with patriotism and progress," wrote the *Oakland Tribune*, "before pollution and snarled traffic made them unwelcome. . . . What had begun as the 'pride and joy' of state highway planners quickly [would] become the freeway that few wanted to drive."[3]

Some argue that was because the city was built before zoning ordinances and land-use laws; others say it is because the community was nonwhite. According to the *Oakland Tribune*, in the 1950s "Alameda County officials did not want to displace too many of the neighborhood's industries because they were important to the job and tax base. The Victorians that were leveled, however, were of little concern. They were occupied by poor blacks, who had no clout."[4] There were few on or off ramps in West Oakland, suggesting the Cypress was built not to benefit local residents, but to insulate travelers from them.

Other intrusions into West Oakland followed: a BART station, a regional U.S. Postal Distribution Center, recycling and baking factories, the Port of Oakland, and assorted truck-related industries. The businesses increased the wear and tear of urban life on the community.

A NEED TO DEFEND ITSELF

West Oakland has a glorious and tumultuous past marked by able civic leaders, a search for social justice, and economic isolation. This legacy, far too extensive to capture here, includes C. L. Dellums, a protégé of the legendary A. Philip Randolph, founder and leader of the Brotherhood of Sleeping Car Porters (the first black union), basketball superstar Bill Russell, and baseball great Frank Robinson. Long before the more privileged students at nearby Berkeley began their battle for free speech and civil

---

[3]*Oakland Tribune*, October 22, 1989.
[4]*Ibid.*

liberties, West Oakland was working to identify and address its social inequities. As time passed, this effort would blend high levels of hope, frustration, and, ultimately, discontent.

In the sixties, West Oakland would become home to the Black Panthers. Started as an effort to recapture their neighborhood, the party would make the names of Huey P. Newton and Angela Davis infamous. And the Panthers themselves would be remembered largely for their call to arms.

The 1970s were a turbulent time. Manufacturing across America was in decline. Urban communities were being abandoned. Those who had the means fled to the suburbs, and those who stayed behind were ridiculed and scorned. Across America, urban areas were in revolt against the construction and expansion of new freeways, treating them as noisy, dusty, dark, and divisive. What was Caltrans, the state department of transportation, to do? Traffic was increasing and few roads were being built. No one wanted a freeway in their backyard. By the 1980s, Caltrans was mainly tinkering around the edges of the state transportation system.

THE BIG QUAKE
LOMA PRIETA: OCTOBER 17, 1989

On Tuesday, October 17, 1989, a television audience estimated at 60 million baseball fans from the United States and around the world were watching the pregame broadcast of the third game of the 1989 World Series. It was San Francisco's version of the old New York subway series. The Oakland A's were pitted against the San Francisco Giants at Candlestick Park. Workers on both sides of the bay had left work early to catch the beginning of the game. At 5:04 p.m., their screens went black.[5] When power was restored . . . the world learned that a quake measuring 7.1 on the Richter scale had just occurred and though its epicenter was about 80 miles south of Oakland, damage was extensive throughout the Bay Area.[6]

In less than a minute, dozens were killed or mortally injured and 3,700 were hurt in the third most lethal earthquake in U.S. history. Forty-two people died when the double-decked Cypress Freeway collapsed. Oakland

---

[5]U.S. Department of Transportation Public Roads, "Replacing Oakland's Cypress Freeway," March 13, 1998.

[6]*Ibid.*

auto mechanic Richard Reynolds recalled: "[I felt] a ripple. [Then I heard] a neighbor screaming . . . [I felt] the whole goddamn ground lifting up. . . . As the sidewalk buckled beneath my feet and [I] looked up . . . a mile-long section of the freeway's upper deck began to heave, then collapsed onto the lower roadway, flattening cars as if they were beer cans. It just slid. It didn't fall. It just slid. You couldn't see [anything] . . . but dust. [Some] people came out of the dust. But not many."[7]

The Cypress Viaduct in West Oakland was hit by a force of at least 2 million tons producing both sideways and up-and-down movement.[8] In a matter of seconds, the section of I-880 between 7 and 18 Street in West Oakland was destroyed while the segment between 18 Street and 34 Street was badly damaged. Property losses were estimated at $7 billion.[9]

CALTRANS

The 1950s were a time of explosive highway expansion. Caltrans engineered and built these increasingly elaborate behemoths and was responsible for making sure that California's roads and freeways worked smoothly and safely. It was time-consuming and expensive, but an easy political sell. "It was rare that the state said no to what Caltrans wanted," said Pete Hathaway, of the California Transportation Commission. "People wanted roads so that is what Caltrans gave them."[10]

Before the earthquake, more than 160,000 vehicles used the elevated, eight-lane Cypress Freeway every day. With the Cypress out of service, I-880 traffic shifted to other parts of the Oakland freeway network, causing heavy congestion. Caltrans was responsible for cleaning up the mess. Roads had to be reopened and traffic restored.

One of the first officials on the scene was project manager Irene Itamura. "We were told early estimates that for every day the Bay Bridge and the Cypress Freeway were down, the Bay Area was losing $1 million dollars a

---

[7]*Ibid.*

[8]*Sacramento Bee*, "A Crushing Quake—California Learned a Lesson from Bay Area Temblor," October 17, 1999.

[9]U.S. Department of Transportation Public Roads, "Replacing Oakland's Cypress Freeway," March 13, 1998.

[10]Phone interview with Pete Hathaway, Wednesday, April 12, 2000.

day," said Itamura. "Caltrans had one mission and that was to replace this freeway as quickly as possible. . . . It was going to be chaotic in the Bay Area with this missing link."[11]

The first goal was to restore the local street system. The second was to rebuild this critical link in the freeway system. "We had to get this project done soon and done on time. We were under pressure. The race was on because we were competing with projects across the Bay," said Itamura.[12] Caltrans was not known for being on time and under budget. Now it had to be. It was also not known for being sensitive to communities, especially minority ones. But this time the world was watching.

"Caltrans was used to dealing with other government agencies; this time it had to deal with everyone," said Jeff Georgevich of the Metropolitan Transportation Commission. "Local constituents were going to vote on this one . . . so local political leaders stayed away. This left Caltrans dangling on its own."[13]

A CITIZEN RESPONSE TEAM

Three days after the earthquake, Ralph Williams, Myra Woods, Gloria Taylor, William Love, Rev. Bishop Johnson, Chappell Haynes, Rev. Will Herzfeld, Gay Plair Cobb, William Coburn, Marcie Miller, Lorna Jones, Rev. Ray Williams, and Jack Atkin met in the home of Paul Cobb to organize a Citizens Emergency Response Team (CERT).[14] Love and Cobb had spent the past three days organizing citizen rescue efforts. The community was ready.

"CERT was not the usual ad hoc citizens advocacy group because most of us had directly suffered from the major construction projects," said Cobb. "Our families had unsuccessfully fought to stop the Cypress Freeway from

---

[11]Phone interview with Irene Itamura, Caltrans District office (Sacramento), Tuesday, April 18, 2000.

[12]*Ibid.*

[13]Interview with Jeff Georgevich at Metropolitan Transportation Commission office (Oakland), Wednesday, April 19, 2000.

[14]*Oakland Tribune*, "Neighbors work to reunite West Oakland after quake," Sunday, October 10, 1997.

being built in the 1950s because it would cut us off from each other."[15] They were not going to lose a second time. In their eyes, enough damage had been done. "It was a movement of people to make sure West Oakland got its fair share of rescue dollars; [we wanted a] guarantee that we [would] not get shafted with another misplaced freeway; and [we wanted] to reunite the West Cypress community with the rest of West Oakland," said Cobb, a West Oakland community leader.[16]

Within weeks, County Supervisor Warren Widener and his wife Mary joined the group and became leaders within CERT. Widener, a former Berkeley mayor, was chosen to coordinate government relations. Several other community leaders including Carol Ward-Allen, former port CEO Walter Abernathy, David Glover, OCCUR's director, were given positions in CERT.[17] They gave CERT something most neighborhood organizations lack. "They [brought] sophistication and expertise to access government, labor, neighborhoods, foundations, and private sectors," said Paul Cobb. "We came to the Loma Prieta/Cypress aftermath with a hope-to-die attitude of never again."[18]

POLITICAL LANDMINE

Historically, federal and state highways have disproportionately impacted poor and minority communities. The original Cypress Freeway forced local politicians to deal with a divided West Oakland community. Whether it was crime, poverty, traffic, or fragmentation, West Oakland had long felt slighted. A political backlash was simmering, and Loma Prieta turned up the heat. The seismic shock waves had turned political, and national television raised the profile.

Memories of Loma Prieta conjured horrific images of collapsing buildings, dust, and dead bodies. The images conveyed a clear message that it had occurred in a poor, predominately African-American community. It was a huge disaster. Fixing it was not going to be easy or cheap, and

---

[15]*Ibid.*

[16]*Ibid.*

[17]*Oakland Tribune*, "CERT leaders express their relief about flyover," November 7, 1999.

[18]*Ibid.*

someone had to pay the price. West Oakland had not had to deal with an elevated freeway that served the needs of others when it was standing, but that now had been transformed into a disaster. Who built the freeway? Who created the risk? Who should bear the consequences? The obvious answer was Caltrans.

Federal legislation provided $1 billion in emergency relief funds for damage to the federal transportation system caused by the earthquake. Major projects eligible for funding included the Embarcadero Freeway, the Central Freeway, and I-280 in San Francisco and the Cypress Viaduct. To qualify for emergency relief, a project had to obligate its funding within three years. But any replacement had to meet modern design standards.[19]

The Cypress structure was designed in the mid 1950s and did not meet current building and safety codes. Caltrans had to make a decision: Should it rebuild the freeway in its current location or look for alternatives. This proved more difficult than first imagined. "There were dozens of places within the process from which someone could say no," said Pete Hathaway of the California Transportation Commission. "All it would take is one of the many involved to delay construction; Caltrans had to negotiate if they wanted to be done on time."[20]

BUDGET CONSTRAINTS

The early 1990s were a time of deep recession in California, and Caltrans lost 3,000 engineers and technicians during the administrations of Governors Deukmejian and Wilson. Caltrans knew that despite the cuts, there would be no sympathy for them. Caltrans had to act quickly.

A union of state engineers blamed Deukmejian. By cutting budgets and refusing to hire staff, they said, he made it impossible to bolster all of the state's bridges. Whoever was to blame, Governor Wilson would have to clean it up. That meant Caltrans had to deal with it.

State officials knew that the freeway was heavily used. It had to be rebuilt. "Bay Area political leaders were determined that Caltrans not dip into the region's transportation budget." said Jeff Georgevich of the Metropolitan Transportation Commission. "They were not going to let this

---

[19]Pete Hathaway.
[20]*Ibid.*

money slated for regional transportation improvements be spent on fixing a freeway in West Oakland."[21]

"Caltrans was expected to meet the deadline necessary to qualify for federal emergency dollars. We had three years in which to obligate the money. Time was short for a project this complex," said Itamura. To qualify for $1 billion dollars in federal aid, Caltrans had to reach agreement in a short period of time or risk having no financing for reconstruction.

"As we were looking at estimates in San Francisco, the cost [kept going] up and up for fixing the Embarcadero Freeway, and the 280 and the 101 exits," said Georgevich. "Caltrans is doing the best it can, but it's not clear that we have enough money to do all these projects." Caltrans would not know until 1993 whether the agency had enough money to rebuild.

THE FEDERAL HIGHWAY ADMINISTRATION

Although California was important to the powers-that-be in Washington, the Federal Highway Administration didn't want to set a precedent. If they sent too much money to California, other states would notice. FHWA decided to send some of its own people to California to protect the bottom line and to reiterate the importance of meeting the deadline if Caltrans wanted to qualify for emergency funds. That meant building the safest and most cost-effective freeway option available. "These were a bunch of old white guys who were here to focus on the bottom line," said Georgevich. "They were not ready for the ardent support and advocacy of this community. . . . Members of the community were saying the freeway was a 'threat to the future of their children.' . . . The [FHWA guys] could not handle it."[22]

The pressure was on because Caltrans had project managers trying to build consensus in San Francisco. Most people expected San Francisco to get its act together and compete to have its freeways rebuilt with emergency money.[23] A billion dollars was not enough to rebuild three freeways. The pot of emergency money was limited, and Congress was not likely to fund all

---

[21]Jeff Georgevich.

[22]*Ibid.*

[23]San Francisco's controversial Mayor Art Agnos knocked down the city's massive Embarcadero Freeway instead of replacing it. The freeway removal was the catalyst for a major revitalization of San Francisco's waterfront.

the reconstruction projects. Time was ticking and Caltrans had already met some resistance.[24]

PART I: CONFRONTATION

In the wake of the Loma Prieta quake, Caltrans engineers planned as they routinely do after a disaster. They focus on clean up and replacement. They sketch designs and calculate cost-estimates. Their job is to come up with the most cost-effective alternatives. So they did. Since city council approval was needed, project manager Irene Itamura knew she needed to gain the support of the West Oakland community. This time the city council would not move without community support. Arrangements for a massive public meeting in the early part of January 1990, were under way. The meeting was to be held at Prescott Elementary School—blocks from the dusty and mangled monument of the fallen freeway.

At the public hearing, armed with sketches and engineering rationale, Itamura argued for a four- or six-lane expressway, with frontage roads along the Cypress corridor, until a permanent replacement could be built. This meant widening the freeway and routing traffic along the large side roads beside the fallen Cypress until the replacement freeway could be rebuilt.

Several community residents rose to denounce the proposal. Then, CERT made its carefully coordinated presentation. Supervisor Warren Widener made a counterproposal to build a permanent freeway over the top of the Southern Pacific Railroad tracks around the outskirts of West Oakland. "We adamantly oppose any kind of an interim freeway along the Cypress corridor because we know that any interim freeway will become permanent," said Widener. "Once it is built, Caltrans will not be able to find the money to replace it."[25]

Community meetings can quickly break down into arguments and bickering. With a prolonged lack of consensus, everyone can easily become frustrated—especially when they feel their presence makes not a whit of difference. Caltrans had made a mistake; it was not adequately prepared. It had the drawings and the numbers, but it had failed to talk and, more

---

[24]Pete Hathaway.

[25]*Oakland Tribune*, "CERT leaders express their relief about flyover," November 7, 1999.

importantly, listen to the community prior to the meeting. If it had, it would have realized how much the community distrusts the "engineer-type" that had put the freeway there in the first place. If it had, it would have realized how project manager Itamura's response—"The interim facility does not, I repeat, does not have any bearing on where the permanent facility will be built."—was precisely the wrong one. "The community did not believe her."[26]

The meetings stretched on for months. Different groups, larger groups, emerged. Everyone represented a group, and everyone received an audience. Politicians and local officials were falling all over themselves to lead the next panel, the definitive one. But time was passing, and the deadline was looming.

Responding to the community upheaval, Caltrans formed the state-local Cypress Reconstruction Advisory Committee to give the community, the county, and the state a role; but consensus seemed unattainable. The Oakland City Council finally forced Caltrans' hand by passing a pair of resolutions opposing any construction in the existing corridor. This meant that Caltrans, in order to gain council approval, had to formally consider all the alternatives. Two of the 16 came to the fore. The first was Widener's proposal. The second was a Caltrans proposal to place an underground corridor along the same route as the fallen Cypress Freeway. By then, West Oakland so distrusted Caltrans that it did not want the Cypress in its neighborhood in any form.

PORT OF OAKLAND

The Port of Oakland is a colossus. It is one of the world's premier ports, a multibillion dollar business, and a political powerhouse. Alignment was not going to happen at the expense of the port. The port was expanding its operations, and its shipping clients strongly supported it. With only modest local competition across the Bay, its real concerns were Long Beach to the south and Seattle to the north. No local official was going to get in its way. The community suggestion to use Middle Harbor Road was not palatable. But using the railroad rights of way might not be a burden to the port—even if it impinged slightly on the capacity of freight trains and on the competition

---

[26]Jeff Georgevich.

among the railroads. Competition among the railroads was important to the port because it lowered charges to shipping companies that used the port. "Sealand and Matson wanted to see more competition among the railroads, it meant better business for them," said Itamura.[27]

Truck traffic was sometimes gridlocked at the port and needed relief. A billion dollars of emergency relief money was not to be sneezed at. It presented an opportunity for the port to improve its efficiency. And it didn't hurt to improve one's community image.

By the late 1980s, the railroads were in decline, but still powerful in political circles. Competition was fierce and business was tight. Reminiscent of yesteryear, the companies preferred to negotiate behind closed doors. Decisions were made with handshakes and community input was usually ignored. To improve profits, the railroads needed to expand and reconfigure their operations to make them more efficient. But it was expensive. In order to deal with their own dilemma, they were willing to listen to Caltrans.

The negotiations were difficult. None of the three companies wanted to give any of the other railroad companies a competitive advantage. "Caltrans had to make concessions with all of them. They each had a price, and we knew that price was going to be expensive. One regret I have is not knowing that only one of the three railroad companies was going to remain years later," said Itamura.[28]

PART II: ALTERNATIVES

Widener would prove instrumental in helping CERT form partnerships, and political coalitions. "Widener . . . understood how to get a bureaucrat's attention," said Cobb. CERT needed its own technical experts, someone Caltrans would not question. Widener proposed that CERT use the same consultants Caltrans used. Would they do it? Not only were they willing to provide alternative routes and engineering rationales, they agreed to do it for free.[29]

---

[27]Irene Itamura.

[28]*Ibid.*

[29]Irene Itamura disputes this version of the existence of alternative submissions by consultants. Note to the case editor submitted 6-12-00.

Next, CERT needed to exploit the fact that the world was watching. So Widener and the California Trucking Association arranged to meet with White House and Department of Transportation officials. They had come to make the case for rerouting Cypress. Widener helped the community and labor leaders navigate the bureaucracy.

Finally, while Widener was doing his part, CERT leaders Abernathy and Ward-Allen arranged to meet regularly with railway companies and the port to assure them that they would benefit from the rerouting plan. CERT's efforts were beginning to pay off. They had opened doors for Caltrans to negotiate. The port, the railroads, and others were listening.[30]

To help communicate with the community groups, Caltrans brought into the process, from its headquarters, an African-American woman. Assigned to develop the transportation plan during reconstruction, particularly for bus and rail supplements, she was perceived as less of an engineering type than Irene Itamura. Whether that was so, and whether she was more sensitive to the kind of community that West Oakland is, are strengths that exist, or not, in the eyes of the beholders. But the comfort level with, and the perception of what is beheld can be important in a politicized environment.

The choice was made to reroute the freeway around West Oakland. Widener's proposal won out. But the work was far from done. Caltrans, despite having a pact with all the players had to fast-track its environmental process. They had only a year left before the deadline on the emergency relief money would pass.[31]

CLEANING UP

In some circles, West Oakland was a fragmented community that continually whined about issues. Although most agreed that the community had seen its share of pollution, there was not necessarily agreement on how to address the problem. There were idealists, realists, angry folks, people with axes to grind, and some that simply wanted help repairing their homes from the quake. Environmental racism was a concern; a cancer causing gas was known to exist in the roadway relocation area. Exposure over a period of years could cause cancer of the liver, nervous system, and lymph nodes.

---

[30]*Ibid.*
[31]Irene Itamura.

When, in the late summer of 1993, a freeway pact was finally signed, no one could recall when so many different groups benefited from the initiatives of a single community-based group. West Oakland was awarded $350,000 for a study and a community transportation plan. Caltrans would pay more than $100 million to (the merged and renamed) Santa Fe Pacific to acquire the train tracks below the freeway. "There have been so many expenses associated with mitigating this thing, it's unbelievable. . . . We've had so many nuisance suits I can't remember them all. You talk about being good neighbors, we've done everything," said Steve Williams.

Because the project cut through one corner of the Postal Service parking lot, Caltrans agreed to build a whole new parking garage. It also agreed to run a job-training program for West Oakland residents, relocate 11 businesses and homes, rebuild BART structures, and install extra insulation and air conditioning at a local church.

The city of Emeryville took Caltrans to court over the Cypress solution, until it agreed to provide for the city increased and direct interchange access. This helped spur ongoing development in the area surrounding Emeryville.

THE MANDELA PARKWAY COMMITTEE

The goal of a Mandela Parkway Corridor Study was to provide the framework for bringing the community together by developing the street and park into a first-class resource. The $350,000 approved and won by the Community of West Oakland would not be enough. With money to hire only minimal staff, the work stretched on for years. It was a disaster in the making. To rescue the project, the city staff formed another advisory committee—to identify proper reuse of the old Cypress Corridor. Where a freeway had stood, a barren strip of land remained. There was a range of ideas from in-filling the area for increased development and housing to recreational areas and beautification; but no consensus. West Oakland did not want to get into a long drawn-out planning process, but it did.

"I know it seems like a long time and the community is frustrated," said Michelle Hightower, project manager for the Mandela Parkway Landscape

Project. "But when you think about it, it's not been as long as people really think. It's a big project."[32]

The next question was who was going to pay for landscaping improvements. Caltrans did not want to. It had already agreed to the $350,000. CERT members on the advisory committee reconnected with their old political allies and pressed Caltrans for additional funds.[33] With a coalition that included County Supervisor Carson and state Senator Don Perata, Oakland won an additional $11.5 million from Caltrans to complete the median project. "I'd say there is a shared responsibility," said George Burtt, vice-president and founder of the West Oakland Commerce Association, "Caltrans is a very, very large rock. If we get enough of us together, we can push on the rock and the rock will move. But it takes a lot of extraordinary effort to get that rock to move."[34] To date, despite the money, only minor change has occurred. Caltrans has said it will have the improvements completed by the autumn of 2001.

OPENING THE CYPRESS FREEWAY

Nearly nine years after the massive Loma Prieta earthquake, Caltrans opened the final link of the Cypress Freeway at a cost of $1.2 billion. Being a good neighbor had proved costly to Caltrans. The collapsed freeway was rebuilt at a cost of $4,000 per inch. Instead of slicing through West Oakland, Caltrans bought a new right-of-way and a list of concessions.

A decade is a long time to wait for a rebuilt freeway. A collapsed segment of the Bay Bridge was repaired in a month. After the Northridge earthquake, a freeway in Santa Monica was completed in a little over two months. Whether a decade was a reasonable amount time to rebuild the Cypress freeway will give rise to a diverse range of opinions.

"Its infuriating," fumed Assemblyman Don Perata, former Alameda County supervisor, now state senator. "One of the few things in my political

---

[32]*Oakland Tribune*, "Quake Damaged Oakland Still Waiting on Mandela Renaissance," October 13, 1999.

[33]Interview with Michelle Hightower at CEDA (Oakland), Wednesday, April 19, 2000.

[34]*Oakland Tribune*, "Quake Damaged Oakland Still Waiting on Mandela Renaissance," October 13, 1999.

life that has made me perpetually angry has been that damn freeway . . . it was one of the gross failures of political leadership that really became obvious."

"If there was a loser in this, despite relocating the freeway, the West Oakland community did not see its vision of economic revitalization come to fruition," said Jeff Georgevich, Metropolitan Transportation Commission.[35]

According to the southern California press, "Some community activists have argued that the construction process has not given enough jobs to the financially strapped city across the bay from San Francisco. Others bemoan the fact that the freeway still plagues the residential fringes of the neighborhood, that promised sound walls may be temporary, that hazardous wastes still need to be cleaned up."[36]

After the Northridge earthquake, Los Angeles Mayor Richard Riordan commented unfavorably on the process used in the Cypress reconstruction efforts: "Why the hell should we have to go out and get consensus?" Riordan asked. "I'm a leader and I have to make decisions. I know people wanted to have [our] freeway fixed and fixed fast. . . . [A]t that first meeting with Caltrans, I made them go for it and not worry about who doesn't like the way they were working."[37]

"All the time we hear, 'Gee, they did it quicker in southern California, but that is a totally different story,'" said Terry Roberts, Oakland's director of public works. "That's not even comparing apples and oranges; its comparing apples and baseballs."[38]

Loma Prieta revamped the state's transportation priorities. Only the next big quake will determine if California has prepared well enough. "Loma Prieta has to rank as one of the defining transportation moments in the history of California," said Caltrans press secretary Jim Drago. "Not just in the Bay Area but all over the state."[39] The major concern for the state agency is whether it has created a precedent it cannot afford to keep up with.

The national taxpayer paid for the mitigations, the reconstruction, and the eventual rerouting of the freeway. Whether this was an appropriate use

---

[35]Jeff Georgevich.

[36]*Los Angeles Times*, July 23, 1997.

[37]*San Francisco Chronicle*, July 21, 1997.

[38]*Ibid.*

[39]*San Francisco Chronicle*, October 16, 1999.

of emergency repair funding is a question with no easy answer. Many interests rose to be major players in the negotiations to reroute the Cypress Freeway. Was it worth it?

"[The Cypress] divided the community," said Bill Love of CERT. "The people in West Oakland were literally cut off from downtown. This is sweet. We moved a freeway. How many people can say that they have moved a freeway?"

Case 6

INTRODUCTION

In *Let the Games Begin*, you have a situation in which people were clearly of (at least) two minds: An overwhelming majority in California expressed itself clearly in favor of tougher treatment of criminals. Yet, a California, and national, audience of the popular *60 Minutes* television program was horrified by what it saw occurring behind California prison walls—along with the prospect that, because of a press blackout, far worse might be happening.

Whether or not the situation depicted in *60 Minutes* reflected the true situation at Corcoran State Prison at the time the case was written is not what the case is about. In fact, a jury found, after brief deliberation, that there was insufficient evidence to convict the four correctional officers accused of having deliberately caused, for their own amusement, the deadly turmoil exposed on tape. If it, or anything like it, could have happened, the importance of media access to prisoners and their conditions is clear. Others argue that access is inconsistent with the need to maintain order in a correctional institution.

Consider the dilemmas facing the various actors drawn to the issue. Was the author of the legislation selected because of his deep and abiding civil liberties credentials? How did his authorship compare with his political image? What was the position of the governor, and should it have affected the author's thinking?

What reputation problem burdened the media in making their case that the violence behind prison walls had to be exposed? How did it empower the Department of Corrections in questioning press motives? What evolving public attitudes might have burdened the case for access?

What was surprising about the position taken by the correctional officers union? Why was the governor, their chief beneficiary and benefactor, willing to part company with them? Consider the possible explanation of their respective motives beyond their statements and beyond the immediate issue confronting them.

If you were a rising political star in the California Legislature and had to vote on the proposed legislation, what would you have done? Would you have done the same if faced with a veto override? How would you explain your position to the power groups offended by your vote? To your constituents on the other side of the issue? Would you consider pressuring the author to drop so controversial a measure that the governor said he would veto anyway? Why would you want to have to express yourself on a controversial matter when it would have no effect? Or, would it?

Outside Public View:
Let the Games Begin!

Research and original writing by Nathan A. Paxton

WHAT, NO TUNICS?

Ordinarily, CBS would have been hard pressed to defend itself against the charges of sensationalism leveled in response to the violence displayed on the 60 Minutes program it aired on March 30, 1997. It featured four muscular men. Racially paired and similarly dressed, they circled warily around the narrow space that enclosed them. This was not a classic movie replay of Spartacus or Demetrius and the Gladiators. There were no tridents, nets, maces, swords, or armor. This was not the Coliseum in Caligula's Rome. Entitled "The Deadliest Prison," the segment was filmed in the exercise yard in Corcoran State Prison in California, home of some of the state's worst criminals—the Level Fours.

Yet, implied *60 Minutes*, there were similarities to ancient Rome. The four men had been trained in violence. They knew that they were expected to fight for their survival. They probably knew, because it had happened before, that they were fighting for the entertainment of their captors. Wagers had been placed on the outcome. Winning was everything. It was only when the incentive to disable and destroy turned into the potential for maiming and killing that the guards in the control tower raised their riot guns loaded with wooden blocks, and then their rifles loaded with bullets. One of the fighters, inmate Preston Tate, was shot and killed. According to inmate Anthony James, currently housed in a federal prison, the shot was fired without warning. There were videotapes of the event. In an earlier encounter, a similarly ugly incident, inmate Vincent Taloomis was shot in the neck, rendering him a quadriplegic. Reinforcing the charges made by James and Taloomis were two correctional officers, Lt. Steve Rigg and Officer Richard Caruso.

One can imagine senior anchor Mike Wallace defending his program on grounds that the gladiatorial combat portrayed, which literally resembled a Roman circus, was an essential part of the scandal being exposed. But many viewers, while titillated by the events described, were understandably outraged.

THE DEPARTMENT OF CORRECTIONS

In the wake of the *60 Minutes* controversy, longstanding accusations of systemwide abusive practices by the California Department of Corrections began to surface. The allegations were like a cancerous tumor, hidden, it was charged, by a systematic cover-up. The media spotlight finally focused on a CDC regulation adopted officially in 1997 that narrowed, and sometimes denied, press access to inmates, reversing a policy of more liberal access that had been in effect for two decades. Previously, face to face interviews with inmates were arranged subject to reasonable limitations, and requests were almost never denied. Recording devices were usually allowed. According to media representatives, the CDC would no longer allow them to interview inmates in any situations that might prove embarrassing to the Wilson administration. In the few cases they were allowed personal access, reporters claimed they were prevented from carrying even pencil and paper, the basic tools of journalism. CDC denied this was their policy but conceded the regulations may not be uniformly enforced throughout its 31 institutions. Worse still, the press charged, confidential communications from inmates to the media were prohibited, raising fears of possible retaliation against inmates who provide information critical of CDC.

In fact, the new limitation had unofficially been in force since late 1995, before it went through the hearing and approval process required by California law. According to reporters, there was no written copy of the rules during the hiatus that would allow anyone to determine whether they were in violation. What had so emboldened this massive bureaucracy that it set caution aside?

Far ahead of growth in the general population, CDC will have increased *tenfold* over roughly a quarter century from 1977 to 2002. A population of just 20,000 will have grown to some 200,000 in what is already the nation's largest prison system. (This does not include incarcerated juveniles or misdemeanor convicts in local jails.) With some 33 institutions, and a budget of more than $5 billion, Corrections will be the largest department in California government.

Determinate sentencing, adopted at the beginning of that period, invited increasingly higher sentences. Then, a tough new "three strikes and you're out" initiative passed under which the third strike can be a nonviolent act. The initiative campaign for its passage relied not on rising crime statistics, but on a pair of grisly, heavily publicized murders. That it was media coverage that may have emboldened CDC is more than a little ironic.

THE OFFICE OF ADMINISTRATIVE LAW

It is said that a civilized society lives by the rule of law rather than the arbitrary dictates of those in power. Laws of general application require the concurrence of two, and sometimes all three, branches of government. Regulations, promulgated by a single agency in the executive branch, may directly, and sometimes harshly, affect the lives of hundreds, thousands, or even millions of people. Such regulations must advance laws adopted through the initiative process or spelled out in the constitution, and they may not conflict with laws adopted by the governor and the legislature. Regulations (except in defined emergencies) must be adopted pursuant to public notice, hearing, and the approval of the courts when challenged. As an added safeguard, regulations are scrutinized by the Office of Administrative Law (OAL) before the courts take jurisdiction. It can toss out a regulation for substantive inconsistency with law or deficiencies in the process through which it was adopted. CDC did not submit its regulation to OAL until April of 1996, and its first submission was rejected. Soon after the regulation was finally promulgated and approved, a federal court challenge was filed by members of the press.

LOBACO'S LOW-BALL

The mild-mannered, but passionate and effective, Sacramento lobbyist for the American Civil Liberties Union, Francisco Lobaco, warily approached the office of one of the leading advocates of law and order. Because Lobaco was going to ask him to carry a measure that could easily be characterized by detractors as "protecting the rights of convicted felons," ACLU did not wish to be known as the sponsor of the bill. Extrinsic controversy—ACLU's initiation of the legislation—should not divert from

CDC's policy "being so fundamentally outrageous . . . that [it] could be sold to members of the Legislature as . . . of the [Communist] Gulag."

KOPP ON THE BEAT

Then-Senator Quentin Kopp is now a Superior Court Judge. While in the legislature, he was regarded as a brilliant and highly skilled, albeit cantankerous, San Francisco Independent. Although he was literally independent, on law and order issues, he was predictably pro law enforcement. His gravelly, booming voice was frequently heard over the hundreds of squawk boxes that pervade the Capitol and nearly every office building in downtown Sacramento. How could Lobaco presume to persuade him to carry the bill?

What Lobaco understood about Kopp was that his need to be heard, his love for debate, and his consequent faith in the wisdom of free speech protections were paramount. Kopp was a lawyer who understood the significance of the First Amendment. He was a part time media host, whose controversy-laden radio talk show was well known to the San Francisco Bay Area. As a consummate politician, he was quite comfortable in dealing with the press.

Not unlike a gladiator preparing for combat, Kopp girded himself to do battle with the CDC. As early as June of 1966, he wrote, in a conservative style meant to appeal to the Republican administration, "Throughout . . . history, the media . . . [have] been responsible for identifying inefficiency, waste, and fraud in government spending. The Department of Corrections is no different than other institutions in terms of such scrutiny. . . . I have not been offered any factual basis linking media access to any intrusion on penological interests."

SB 434 would establish confidential correspondence with the news media as an inmate's civil right in the state. It declared that the free exchange of information "benefits the public and fosters a safe and efficient prison system" and that "there is no legitimate reason for a blanket ban on interviews." It directed the CDC to allow the media to interview prisoners. It applied to state prisons and prisoners only and had no affect on federal prison policy.

As in Congress, bills introduced in the California Legislature must pass two houses before reaching the desk of the chief executive. A bill is referred to one or more policy committees in each house for analysis of the measure's policy effects. Laws do not operate in a vacuum, but interact with often complex and comprehensive bodies of existing law. Analysts identify issues and options for legislative members of the relevant committees to consider. If a bill is determined to have a fiscal effect (that is if it requires the state to spend money), it is automatically referred to the fiscal committee of the house in which it is being heard. Any one of the narrow channels through which a measure must pass—policy committees, appropriations committees, and often subcommittees of very few members—can become a graveyard.

If it survives, it must be approved by a majority of the members of each house—sometimes a two-thirds majority—before it enters the politically volatile domain of the executive. The governor has 30 days from the bill's passage to approve or veto it. If it is approved, the bill becomes a law. A governor's veto is only rarely overridden. It may seem surprising that any legislation ever passes. And, of the thousands that do each year, few deal with extremely controversial issues.

A *PRESS*-ING MATTER

One of the strongest forces in the storm surrounding SB 434 were the lobbyists for the press. The California Newspaper Publishers' Association represents the business people who own and control the operations of a variety of newspapers large and small. The women and men who write the words that fill the pages of newspapers and magazines are represented by the northern California chapter of the Society of Professional Journalists (SPJ), headed by Peter Sussman. Both Kopp's staff and Lobaco considered Sussman integral to the bill's passage.

Sussman brought a decade of experience in prison-media issues to the table. He had been on the *San Francisco Chronicle*'s staff for 29 years, most recently as editor of *Sunday Punch*, a popular weekly section of features and commentary. In that section, he occasionally published pieces by an insightful federal prisoner named Dannie Martin. In 1988, Martin wrote an essay that criticized policies a new warden had introduced. He contended they depersonalized prisoners and heightened tensions in the facility. Two days after the essay was published, Martin was placed in the "hole." The charge was violating a rarely enforced regulation prohibiting federal prisoners from writing news articles under their own name. Sussman filed suit in federal court alleging violations of Martin's and the paper's First Amendment rights.[1]

"STRIKE ONE" AGAINST CDC: 60 MINUTES

Typically, the author presents his or her bill before a committee, the proponents and opponents of the bill offer brief testimony, and the members ask questions of the author and the witnesses. SB 434 was first heard in the Senate Public Safety Committee, composed of five Democrats, two Republicans, and Independent Kopp, who submitted several amendments that strengthened the measure considerably. One amendment broadened the definition of members of the news media to take into account the explosion of nontraditional media outlets, from newsletters to the Internet. Another explicitly directed CDC to allow reporters to use the "tools of the trade." SB 434 supporters assured members that with increased scrutiny there would be no threat to security of the system. "It has the logical qualifiers based on the public safety and on the security of the facility," Kopp said.

Was it a coincidence that the bill was heard and approved just two days after 60 Minutes aired "The Deadliest Prison"? Sussman pointed out dramatically that CDC policy nearly prevented the 60 Minutes story, and that it would have deprived lawmakers of precisely the kind of information they needed. "The department says . . . we can get information from prisons . . . by rumor," communicating with prisoners through their family and friends. "The most dangerous thing that can happen in a prison is [to rely on] rumor." Supporters noted that even CDC estimated the press made only 100-200 requests for face-to-face interviews per year, an average of six or seven per prison—an insignificant burden. Media sources believed the number was much smaller.

"STRIKE TWO" AGAINST CDC: DON NOVEY AND CCPOA

That the press, civil libertarians, mental health, AIDS and prisoner rights groups were the core of the coalition supporting SB 434 surprised no one.

---

[1]For further information on the Martin case, see Dannie Martin and Peter Sussman, *Committing Journalism: The Prison Writings of Red Hog* (New York: W. W. Norton, 1993).

When the California Labor Federation joined them, it was somewhat unexpected. But the first real surprise was the support of the powerful and politically unpredictable California Correctional Peace Officers Association. CCPOA represents the correctional officers (the term prison guard is strenuously resisted and resented) who work in daily contact with inmates. Viewed by Capitol insiders as a law-and-order police group, they were seen as close allies of Gov. Wilson, CDC, and Republicans generally. At the hearing, the colorful and enigmatic CCPOA leader, Don Novey, took a seat next to Francisco Lobaco and the ACLU. The committee chair, Sen. John Vasconcellos, took note of the extraordinary picture. But Novey had his reasons—actually several of them.

According to Ryan Sherman, one of CCPOA's lobbyists, denying the media access to the prisons would prevent the public from seeing the sort of people CCPOA's members dealt with on a daily basis. Sherman added, "If the media can find the bad apples in our membership and get them out, that's good," for the CCPOA and the public.

Novey addressed the hardball politics. "Very rarely do I support a Quentin Kopp bill," Novey said, but "we have not had a security problem with the media in 27 years." Novey was there to make a different point: it was the prison wardens and CDC who were creating the security risks by covering up. Novey told the committee that the chapter president at Corcoran State Prison was threatened with disciplinary action if he dared to discuss prison management issues—especially problems of safety that directly affected the guards. If there were problems, the media were the officers only hope. Novey had come to the hearing to show the prison wardens, and the CDC, that despite longstanding affection for the governor, correctional officers would not be pushed around. CDC was effectively isolated.[2]

---

[2]This would remain the case until late summer, when a couple of victims' rights groups would join the opposition to SB 434. CDC legislative liaison said that he had talked to the victim groups and asked if they would look at the bill and consider joining the opposition. (This is a standard practice in the California legislative process.)

DOWN BUT NOT OUT

CDC argued that the measure had nothing to do with the press' right to report what was going on in the prison system, because there were other ways the press could gain information from prisoners. "We have no problem with [the public's right to know]." The problem is that "this measure bolsters inmate rights," said Mike Neal, CDC's legislative liaison.

The first committee critic of the measure was Democratic Senator Adam Schiff, a former U.S. Attorney. He, like CDC, was concerned that interviewing inmates on camera would increase their notoriety. Seeing inmates on camera would "re-victimize the victims"—force them to relive the pain associated with the crime experience. It would increase the esteem of some of the worst and most manipulative inmates among their admiring peers within the prison. The big wheels would then turn this power against the prison authorities. Schiff said he would support the bill if it could be made to prohibit the use of video recording devices.

CDC'S "THIRD STRIKE"

The polite but tense atmosphere of the committee hearing broke at one point. As Senate President John Burton spoke to Tip Kindel, the CDC's media spokesman, Kindel began to shake his head at the Democratic senator. Burton lost his temper and yelled at Kindel, "Don't shake your head at me like that! You don't want to mess with me!"

After extraordinarily lengthy discussion, the committee voted. SB 434 received six affirmative votes, four from Democrats, one from Kopp, and one from Republican Bruce McPherson, a former newspaper publisher. Schiff voted against the bill, as did Republican Richard Rainey.

RETRENCHMENT AND COUNTER-ATTACK

Though it focused on the expansion of inmate rights in the Senate Public Safety hearing, CDC later offered several other arguments against Kopp's bill. They continued to maintain that the changes in CDC policy were not really substantive. In an interview roughly a year after the Senate Public Safety hearing, CDC representatives Neal and Kendall said, "There's nothing in the system [a reporter] can't get. A good reporter can get the story they want." All CDC had really done, they contended, was take away a

86

reporter's convenience, something to which the media had no right. Neal also argued that the media were not even-handed in their portrayal of convicts, often glorifying them and their misdeeds. "If news programs would give equal time to victims, this policy might not have arisen," he said.

In a well-formulated legal attack, CDC claimed it had long had the highest court in the land on its side. The United States Supreme Court, in a California case involving the CDC—*Pell v. Procunier*—decided 20 years ago that the First Amendment does not guarantee the public or the press a right to obtain information. It added that journalists have no greater rights of access than the general public; and, that the public's need for access to information will be balanced against other social needs, such as law enforcement interests and personal privacy.[3]

In a political counter-offensive, CDC maintained that only a few years earlier the legislature itself had reaffirmed its power to adopt legitimately restrictive policies. In 1994, then-Senator Robert Presley (currently director of Corrections under Governor Davis)—keeping with the California electorate's sentiment that prison punishment was too soft—obtained passage of a measure that spelled out criteria applicable to a body of law known as the "Inmate Bill of Rights." A key change allowed CDC to use "legitimate penological interests" to justify denial of certain privileges. Relying on the language, CDC curtailed, or removed privileges relating to mail, recreation, grooming, and, now, media access. According to Kopp, however, Sen. Presley had stated for the record that he did not intend that his bill would be used to curtail media access to prisons.

BOTH SIDES NOW

Senator Kopp believed that bipartisan support was necessary to make sure the bill passed and the governor signed it. He also thought it important to have Republican votes to overcome the loss of votes from conservative Democrats who objected to it. On May 12, Kopp amended the bill, tweaking definitions and adding Senator McPherson as a co-author. Previous co-authors had all been liberal Democrats—Senator Vasconcellos and San Francisco Assembly Member Carole Migden. Before the bill came up for

---

[3]Charles Davis, "Outside, Looking In: Covering America's Prisons" (Unpublished manuscript: Southern Methodist University, 1998), 4.

debate on the floor, Randall Henry, the Kopp staff member working on SB 434, met with Republican Ray Haynes' staff. Haynes' office prepares the Republican floor analyses of bills, and without a favorable analysis, SB 434 would attract few, if any, Republican votes. The result of the meeting was a change in the definition of a media representative, to include only "bona fide journalists."

On May 15, Kopp took up the measure for debate on the floor. He outlined the situation that gave rise to the legislation, how the bill would change current policy, and tried to clear up any misconceptions members might have about his measure. Then he sat down and prepared for his closing speech.

Lengthy debate on any measure is unusual in the California Senate. With thousands of bills to consider each year, those without opposition are passed "on consent" (i.e., adopted without debate or discussion). Others are discussed for a few minutes. For a bill to receive more than a half hour of the Senate's time, as SB 434 did, demonstrated that it had stirred deeply held convictions. Moreover, while floor debate is not usually viewed as decisive for the resolution of issues—most controversial matters are faced in committee and most members have already made up their minds—a number of members were attracted to the debate precisely because it might be decisive.

Republicans Haynes and McPherson were the first to rise and urge their colleagues to support SB 434. Two Democrats then spoke against it. The first was Majority Leader Charles Calderon, speaking perhaps in anticipation of running for attorney general the next year. Then Adam Schiff rose, declaring that SB 434 was not a First Amendment issue, and stating that his opposition was based on the fact that the bill would allow video recording devices in the prisons.

Other members rose in support, some on long-standing animosity toward the CDC, others on projections of the bill's consequences or on interpretations of how far CDC could go relying upon the standard they had voted for previously, "legitimate penological interest."

Conservative Orange County Republican Ross Johnson rose and offered one of the most eloquent floor speeches given in the entire debate. Coincidentally, it was also one of the shortest. He emphasized every utterance, punctuating each word for effect. "This bill is worthy of support for a very simple reason. A free, democratic society doesn't have anything to fear from a free, unfettered press. Please vote 'aye'."

Kopp then rose to close with what some have described as the most impassioned speech they have ever heard him give. Kopp declared, his voice rising, that if SB 434 was not a First Amendment issue, nothing was.

"For 20 years," he said, "under the Department of Corrections [own] rule, there were no abuses of the conjective, hypothetical, fantasy nature of some TV reporter coming in day after day after day after day. If you want to find a bogeyman, you can find it anywhere." Kopp quoted from a column that appeared on the opinion pages of the conservative *Orange County Register*, written by columnist Linda Seebach: "'Publicity about abuses in the operation and management of the system are deeply embarrassing to the officials concerned. If they make it harder for journalists to find out, there will be less unfavorable publicity.'"

SB 434 needed 21 favorable votes to pass in the 40-member body. It received 23, two more than required. There were eight negative votes and nine abstentions or absences. There were substantial numbers of both parties on each side as well as in the ranks of those who did not vote. A few more Democrats than Republicans supported the measure, while a few more Republicans than Democrats opposed it.

LIKE A ROCK

Governor Pete Wilson's supporters and opponents alike consider him a singularly stubborn man. As Sweet said, "This governor does what he believes in. He doesn't care who his supporters or opponents are. Even if 100,000 people want him to sign a bill, and he doesn't believe in it, he will veto it. Unpopular decisions don't faze him." At the same time, he occasionally surprises his staff and the public with his position on a bill. The general procedure for the governor's staff, in presenting a bill for Wilson's signature, is to go into his office, review the measure, and make a recommendation. Wilson reviews the bill and recommendation and makes his own decision, sometimes going against the recommendations of his staff.

Because the bill passed the Senate, it began to look as if SB 434 might actually land on the governor's desk. Kopp, his staff, and the bill's sponsors communicated with the governor's office to evaluate the prospects of securing Wilson's signature. In late May, Kopp and Henry met with Michael Sweet, one of the governor's deputy legislative secretaries. Kopp got some bad news: Wilson himself was personally responsible for the change in CDC regulations that had inspired the bill. He had become disgusted with seeing prisoners on television treated like celebrities.[4] According to Sweet, it is not unusual for a governor to ask departments or agencies under the purview of the executive branch to change their regulations to suit a policy preference. And, when a department or agency wants to change procedures in a significant way, it must secure the approval of the governor. There seemed little chance that a governor so heavily invested in a position would be willing to admit error and change it.

The chief objection was that the Kopp bill "liberalized" the Inmate Bill of Rights by adding confidential correspondence with the media to the list. Sweet said, "This is a big deal because this Governor is on record as tough on crime." Wilson had previously adamantly supported voter approval of California's "three strikes" law, increased punishment for domestic violence offenses, the removal of conjugal visits for prison inmates, and "Son of Sam" laws (prohibiting inmates from profiting from their crimes). "I know the Governor would never sign such a bill."

Sweet told Kopp he would have to remove the offending section of his bill that dealt with the Inmate Bill of Rights if he wanted any chance of securing approval. "The governor," said Sweet, "gets rabid about this issue." Kopp went back to Sweet, this time accompanied by the bill's supporters—Sussman of SPJ, Lobaco of the ACLU, and Sherman from the CCPOA —to see if they could arrange a compromise that might allow the governor to sign the measure. On May 23, within days of the second meeting with Sweet, Kopp removed the operational portions of the bill from the Inmates' Bill of Rights, but added their equally sensitive equivalent elsewhere as accruing to journalists.

According to Sherman, once the CCPOA discovered that the bill directly opposed a policy the governor set down himself, it knew that the measure could never secure a signature: "We pointed out that there was no need for this bill if the governor was on board. He could just order a change to the regulations." It was the press, he said, who wanted to move the bill forward. CCPOA had gone along because, although they thought that SB 434 was a fundamentally good policy, they hoped their continued support would help them make friends among the media whom they normally did not see as allies.

---

[4]Interview with Tip Kindal, Mike Neal.

IN THE ASSEMBLY

SB 434 passed the Assembly with barely a ripple. It passed in the Assembly Public Safety Committee by 6-2, with all five Democrats and one Republican voting in favor. In the Assembly Appropriations Committee, opponents and proponents trotted out the familiar arguments, the committee members asked the familiar questions, and the measure passed 17-3, with 13 Democrats and four Republicans in favor and three Republicans against.

The Assembly floor session on SB 434 was shorter but no less impassioned than that of the Senate debate four months earlier. When a legislative measure is up for consideration in the opposite house, the author may not present the measure. The member must instead find a "floor jockey"—a member of the other house willing to carry the measure. For SB 434, Assembly Member Migden, who supported the measure from the start, managed the bill on the Assembly floor when it came up for a vote on September 5.

Again, one of the most eloquent comments in favor of the measure came from Tom McClintock, a southern California Republican at least as conservative as Senator Ross Johnson. "Free nations do not hold prisoners incommunicado. As Justice Brandeis said, 'Sunlight is the best of disinfectants.' People are capable of sorting out fact and fiction for themselves."

Opponents of the measure focused on two arguments. Republican Larry Bowler blamed the legislature for trying to micromanage the prison system. He said the measure was supported by the ACLU, "the prisoner rights union." (This was the only supporter of SB 434 he mentioned.) Republican Brett Granlund said that the portion of SB 434 that allowed confidential correspondence with the media would better allow prisoners to run their criminal enterprises outside the prison walls.

Debate was closed, and voting opened with the clang of a bell. Because the Assembly uses an electronic voting system that tallies the votes instantly, displaying the total tally and each member's individual vote on a large light board above the speaker's rostrum, the vote was completed in roughly one minute. SB 434 received 54 ayes (40 Democrats, 14 Republicans), and 19 noes (17 Republicans, two Democrats), an exact two-thirds majority—seemingly significant since that is required, albeit in both houses, to override a governor's veto. Having secured passage, it returned to the Senate for concurrence.

If a measure is changed after it leaves its house of origin and it passes the other house, it must return to the house of origin for concurrence. This means that the house of origin must accept the changes (or get the second house to agree to a compromise) before it passes the bill on to the governor for signature or veto. On September 10, the Senate considered SB 434 for the last time. Kopp rose and said, almost with surprise,[5] that the Assembly amendments had improved the bill. Senator Schiff, who had opposed the bill five months before, said that the amendments had satisfied his objections,[6] and he would vote for the bill. SB 434 passed on a 27-8 vote in the last days of the 1997 legislative year, another two-thirds majority. At 4 P.M. that day, SB 434, having received two-thirds support on both sides, was sent to the governor's office.

In his letter to Wilson seeking approval of SB 434, Kopp highlighted several points: First, the number of interview requests was hardly onerous. Second, SB 434 empowered CDC to establish restrictions on the time, place, and manner of interviews "if it determines the interview will pose a threat." Finally, media interviews, eliminate otherwise necessary reliance on "rumors, innuendo, and sketchy memory," that threaten the safety of prisoners and the tax-paying public's right to know.

Peter Sussman and the other journalists went into overdrive, generating a tidal wave of editorial support from California newspapers large and small. The *Riverside Press-Enterprise,* the *Sacramento Bee,* the *Contra Costa Times,* the *Oakland Tribune,* the *San Francisco Chronicle,* and the *Los Angeles Times* all weighed in. The *Chronicle* summed up the tone of these arguments, saying, "The consequences of this ban are obvious, and they are intolerable in a free society.... The public has a right to know what is going on in these institutions."[7]

---

[5]"Surprise" because the Senate often looks with bemusement on the lower house of the legislature. Above the Senate rostrum is written "*Senatoris Est Civitatis Libertatum Tueri*"—"It is the duty of the Senate to protect the liberties of the people." Senators joke that the Latin phrase really means "It is the duty of the Senate to protect the people from the Assembly."

[6]The amendments, however, did not specifically prevent television cameras from entering the prison system.

[7]"Nothing to Hide, Nothing to Fear," *San Francisco Chronicle,* September 22, 1997, A20.

EPILOGUE

On September 15, at a bill signing ceremony for a piece of victims' rights legislation, Wilson had promised to address SB 434—supposedly to explain his opposition. He made no mention of the measure. Supporters argued there was still a thin reed of hope of avoiding a veto. It was thin, but it was all they had to motivate them. On October 12, Pete Wilson sent a letter to the Senate, vetoing SB 434.

> The purpose of imprisonment is punishment and deterrence of crime. Those that are housed in state prison should not be treated as celebrities. . . . Such attention is a disincentive to inmates to focus upon the remorse that is essential while in prison. . . . The First Amendment does not guarantee the press a constitutional right of special access to information not available to the general public, nor does it cloak the inmate with special rights of freedom of speech.

Senator Kopp did not attempt a veto override, believing it would be a futile effort. He reasoned that Republicans who voted for the measure, although comprising part of the two-thirds support, would not vote against a governor of their own party, especially with another year to go in the legislative session. SB 434 was dead.

III. Intergovernmental Dynamics

Case 7

The late Joe Serna was indeed *A Big Mayor* and, in terms of mayoral empowerment under its municipal charter, Sacramento is indeed *a Little City*. How did a legally weak mayor, by California's municipal standards —who was racked with cancer and died before completing his term— exercise power that reached beyond the official responsibilities of the city? No one, after all, elected him to run the schools. A board of school trustees was voted upon and elected by the people to run the schools. What entitled him to use his personal and official political powers to pressure the school board to change, first, its ways and, later, its membership? What allowed him to divert his time, energy, and attention from municipal problems to educational ones? Could he have escaped criticism by saying "public office does not relieve one of other civic responsibilities?" Would it have been credible? Was he acting as just another private citizen?

Imagine the reaction to his announcement that he was going to organize a recall—although he didn't actually endorse it—of those members of the school board majority that he considered obstructionists! What if the school board had announced it concluded the city was poorly run, that it adversely impacted the schools, and that a recall of the mayor was in order? You can see why Serna's decision was so extraordinary. He had concluded that the future of Sacramento was inevitably linked to a positive educational environment and that it would not happen under the school board's majority. With what aspects of the future of Sacramento did Serna seem most concerned?

Did Serna by his candid—some school board members might say *insulting*—style cause the board to harden in its determination to take a course different than he proposed? Should he have been more sympathetic to their problems—lack of financing for infrastructure, a militant teachers' union, and hyper-diversity in languages spoken and economic backgrounds? What had the first school board done that made it difficult for them to engender sympathy? What became the icon that people inevitably linked to mention of the board?

What led taxpayers—many of them older and with no children in the public schools—to sympathize with the recall? What caused the parent community—including those from minority and poor families—to sympathize with the recall? Why did the business community want to provide resources for what was billed as a program for education reform? What managerial mishaps were they able to observe?

How did the board exploit this business coalition to attempt to defend itself? What other counter-charges did the board majority level and how well did they make their case?

In addition to the readily available negative images of the board prior to replacement of its majority, what positive images did Serna convey about his program? What in Serna's background, municipal goals, relationships, and profession helped make his coalition building and, ultimately, his program successful? Who may have been one of his role models? How is he typical, or atypical, of Latino leadership on the rise? Did his ethnicity help or hurt the recall effort? Why did he not formally endorse it? Following his victory, how did he alleviate fears he would want to continue to control district decisions through his school board "puppets"?

Constructive Squabbling:
A Big Mayor for a Little City

Researched and original writing by Nisha Vyas

HOW ARE THE SCHOOLS?

It was 1995, and Sacramento Mayor Joe Serna, Jr., had a problem. As an advocate for economic development, he was struggling to find ways to boost an economy just pulling out of recession. He pushed the boundaries of his role as mayor by taking an active role in recruiting businesses to Sacramento, and retaining the ones already there. Widely successful in his endeavors, one question from corporate executives and business owners always stumped him: How are the schools? Of the seven school districts in Sacramento, the Sacramento City Unified School District (SCUSD), with over 42,000 students, was the largest. It was also plagued with many of the same problems as other urban schools in California—overcrowding, run-down buildings, lack of supplies, and insufficient credentialed teachers. Schools in the district performed poorly on statewide tests and had high illiteracy and truancy rates. As mayor, Serna had no legal jurisdiction over public schools. Other elected officials—the Sacramento City Board of Trustees, or school board—were charged with making district policy. But they had become targets of growing criticism from the press and the public.

There was the symbolically disastrous purchase of a new administrative building for $8.5 million in downtown Sacramento while city schools limped along with leaking roofs and nonfunctioning bathrooms. Critics dubbed it the "Taj Mahal." There were constant public squabbles with school administrators. There was a poisonously unproductive relationship with the Sacramento City Teachers' Association (SCTA). And, finally, there was an embarrassing lack of civility between competing factions on the board.

Sacramento City Unified School District was, in many ways, typical of California's urban school districts. Social problems intruded increasingly into its educational complex of 42,000 students in 79 schools. There were drugs, and with the drugs came gangs and violence. There were dysfunctional families, and, with them, poverty, hunger, and abuse. Principals and teachers were ill-prepared to deal with multicultural, multilingual, and limited English speaking student bodies.

Sacramento schools had high dropout rates and high rates of illiteracy. The dropout rate for SCUSD high schools was 12 percent, compared to 4.9 percent statewide in 1993-94. In 13 out of 56 elementary schools, it appeared that less than 10 percent of the students were reading at grade level.[1] Fewer than half of district students had mastered the basic skills included in the core curriculum. There was a continuing decline in the percentage of students scoring at or above grade level in seventh grade math, and a corresponding increase in the number unprepared to take algebra. Further along in the middle schools, over 20 percent of the students were not earning passing grades in language arts, math, science, and history, and were unprepared for high school work. There were growing numbers of suspensions in the middle and high school grades, particularly among African-American students.[2]

While the statistics reflected a problem, the numbers themselves did not create a sense of crisis. Community Partners for Educational Excellence (CPEE), a grass-roots organization active in educational policy, tried to spotlight the failures of the school system. But, as Maureen Fitzgerald of CPEE observed, "[People] didn't expect much from the schools, didn't expect kids to do well, and weren't surprised when kids dropped out."[3]

CAN'T WE ALL JUST GET ALONG?

Elected at large and paid $750 a month, school board members oversee the district's administrative operations and expenditures. School districts have unique jurisdictions, overlapping with the territories and constituencies of cities, counties, and other special districts. The overlap can cause tension

---

[1] *Trends and Status 1994: Toward Operational Goals and Beyond.* Prepared by the Accountability Office Staff, Sacramento City Unified School District, August 23, 1994.

[2] *Ibid.*

[3] Maureen Fitzgerald, telephone interview, April 20, 2000.

between governing bodies. Prior to the early 1990s, the school board did not garner much attention. When Michelle Masoner ran for the board in 1989, she noticed that powerhouse organizations like the Chamber of Commerce and the Board of Realtors did not get involved. Neither did Mayor Ann Rudin, except to endorse incumbents.[4]

In 1995, the school board had seven members: Gaspar Garcia, Ida Russell, Virgil Price, Louise Perez, Tom Griffin, Mary Wimberly, and Michelle Masoner. Garcia was elected in 1991. He holds a doctorate in school administration from the University of Southern California. Ida Russell, the president of the board, had served for 11 years. Virgil Price, a former teacher and principal, was elected in 1994. Louise Perez served on the board for 13 years. Tom Griffin is an educational attorney elected in 1994. Masoner, a former special education teacher, served 1994-95 as the board's president after her 1989 election.

Increased focus on the board's actions coincided with the election of Garcia in 1991. "When Gaspar was elected, everything changed. Jo Ann Yee, Garcia, and I were the only board members visiting the schools. Gaspar micromanaged and told schools when he thought they were still screwing up," says Masoner.

The board divided along racial lines, with the people of color (Garcia, Russell, Price, and Perez), except African-American Wimberly, voting as a bloc. Many decisions were made by 4-3 votes. Wimberly, Griffin, and especially Masoner were publicly critical of the "Gang of Four," during board meetings and in the press. Disagreements between Masoner and Russell, and Masoner and Garcia, often turned into personal attacks. In May 1994, when Masoner was president, Garcia told her the board had plans to remove her as president.[5] Unpopular with the majority of the board, she was succeeded by Ida Russell when her term ended.

A previous board, with many of the same members as the 1995 board, had already lost the confidence of many teachers and parents through financial decisions deemed wasteful by community leaders. The 1994 decision to purchase an administrative building at 520 Capitol Mall, remains unpopular, although Garcia still describes the acquisition as a super deal:

---

[4]Michelle Masoner, telephone interview, April 28, 2000.

[5]Carlos Alcala, "City School Board May Dump Its President," *Sacramento Bee*, May 3, 1994, B1.

Our district offices at 16th and N were declared unsafe, so we found the former IBM building at 520 Capitol Mall. It cost $8.5 million and another $1.5 million to refurbish. At the time, we wanted to spend $7.5 million to refurbish the school site at John Morris. We took out a $13.8 million loan and envisioned selling our old skills center (which was filled with asbestos) to [the University of California, Davis or The Shriners] for $10 million, and wanted to sell the property at 16th and N for $2.5 million. We were also going to sell a vacant lot for $700,000. This was all supposed to happen. But the superintendent [Terry Grier] got in the way.[6]

The relationship between a school board and a superintendent sometimes can be contentious. In Sacramento, however, the relationship with Grier was widely regarded as broken. The problems were micromanagement by the board and its overly hasty selection of superintendents. Keith Larick, who served as superintendent from 1986 to 1989, left with a $69,000 contract buyout. Rudy Crew served from 1989 to 1993 and left under a cloud of controversy, ultimately to manage schools in the Pacific Northwest and eventually New York City's public schools. Although there were those who believed he was looking for "a larger pond," many felt the board "chased away a good leader." In between, but for a full 18 months, there was an acting superintendent, whose interim tenure contributed to leadership instability. In June 1994, Terry Grier became superintendent with an expensive and controversial contract.

Union contracts were also controversial, particularly the contract with SCTA. As school board member Jay Schenirer said: "In a dysfunctional system, when you know what you're doing, you can do pretty well. I think [the teachers' union] had done pretty well for a long time."[7]

Hal Stemmler, a member of CPEE wrote in the *Sacramento News and Review*: "[The] district's confrontational relationship with its teachers' union has produced one of the most notorious, dysfunctional, litigious, grievance-infested collective bargaining contracts ever seen."[8] At issue were

---

[6]Gaspar Garcia, telephone interview, April 21, 2000. Michelle Masoner disagrees with Garcia's interpretation of events.

[7]Jay Schenirer, personal interview, April 19, 2000.

[8]Hal Stemmler, "Forget Education," *The Sacramento News and Review*, October 31, 1996, 13.

overdue raises, board secrecy, and continual contract changes. Two recall efforts in 1993 and 1994 targeted the entire board, but quickly fizzled out. In 1994, the *Sacramento Bee* began to focus heavily on the school board's actions and district decision making. The newspaper was already running articles about the state of the public education system. Fitzgerald recalled, "They were having trouble with the unions, and that's always been a perennial challenge for this district.[9] Mayor Joe Serna emerged in that dialogue as a vocal critic of the board and an avid advocate for change.

MEET JOE SERNA

In most of California's cities, including Sacramento, the position of mayor is relatively weak. "Serna had no authority to propose budgets, hand out significant appointments, veto council action or directly manage even the dogcatcher,"[10] said Maureen Fitzgerald.

Joe Serna, Jr., was a professor of government at California State University, Sacramento. He knew the role of a mayor and the rules of "jurisdictional orthodoxies"—the institutional boundaries that limit an actor's movement. But Serna was well-connected, politically savvy, and he was the mayor of Sacramento. As mayor-elect, two months before he took office in 1993, he had parked his car in the spot reserved for the mayor, without any self-conscious feelings about being presumptuous. As the first Latino mayor of a major American city, he instinctively pushed boundaries. He helped keep the National Basketball Associations's Kings, Sacramento's only major sports franchise, in the city by bullying the owner into staying. He developed relationships with influential business leaders in order to promote development and economic growth—an unusual move for a self-described liberal Democrat, former farm worker, and labor organizer. He was described as blunt, intolerant of excuses, whiny, and at times abrasive. He was not afraid to make enemies, evident from his rivalry with controversial, but popular, City Councilman Robbie Waters.

---

[9]Telephone interview, April 20, 2000.

[10]Jeff Raimundo, "The Serna Legend will Challenge Future Mayors," *The Sacramento Bee*, November 9, 1999. Wysiwyg://zoffsitebottom.36/ http://www. sacbee.com/news/special/serna/serna_raimundo.html

In his 1992 campaign, although the mayor and the city had no official role in public education, Serna promised to use the mayor's office as a bully pulpit on education. In his first few months in office, he launched a mayor's summer reading program with the help of local businesses. But, the reading program, and other literacy measures, were overshadowed by board problems.

Gina Montoya was Serna's administrative assistant assigned to education. After Serna was elected and began to discuss education, she said, "We had several private meetings with board members who, off the record, would tell us, 'Look, we can't change the system. These kids are poor kids, they are minority kids, and we can't work with their parents. It is just beyond us; it cannot happen. Why push it? You know this Joe, you're an educator.' That was completely unacceptable to us. Completely unacceptable."[11] Tensions ensued between the board and the mayor. And the groundwork was laid for a turf battle.

Maureen Fitzgerald vividly described a mayoral visit to a school board meeting in early 1995 and Gaspar Garcia's angry reaction at Serna's interference. "He came uninvited into my house and insulted me," said Garcia. "He came and told us how to be better board members. So I told him how he could be a better mayor."[12] When efforts at private collaboration between city hall and the school board failed, Serna went public.

In the August 1995, the mayor convened a 14-member group of business, community, and ethnic leaders and asked them to define the problems the city schools were facing and prescribe solutions. The "Mayor's Commission on Education and the City's Future" was cochaired by Robert Trigg, a respected former superintendent of the Elk Grove Unified School District, and Phil Angelides, a Sacramento businessman, and, at the time, a failed candidate for state treasurer. The first few meetings were closed-door, which prompted complaints from CPEE. While technically, the Brown Act (which says government hearings must be open to the public) did not apply to the commission, the organization felt reform efforts should be discussed in public. As Fitzgerald said, "There's no doubt in my mind that we were right to press them. They may have opened it up eventually if we'd

---

[11]Gina Montoya, personal interview, April 28, 2000.
[12]Gaspar Garcia.

said nothing. . . . [But] you know what I think? That in the beginning meetings, Serna was giving them their marching orders."[13]

By November 1995, the commission had visited schools, held hearings, and listened to testimony from parents, teachers, students, and administrators—all open to the public. Serna presented the document they produced in a November 7 press conference. The report detailed underachievement by educators as well as students, outdated textbooks, poor facilities, and a host of other problems that parents already knew, according to Fitzgerald. The report denounced the board's belligerence, but it was not entirely negative. It outlined recommendations for the board and district administrators focusing on stability and communication.

Just after midnight on November 8, 1995, hours after the report with its recommendations for stability and communication was released, four of the seven members of the school board—Garcia, Russell, Price, and Perez—met behind closed doors and fired Superintendent Terry Grier. The action was widely interpreted as a defiant gesture towards the commission and the mayor. The board members refused to discuss the matter publicly and shut themselves off from the press. *Sacramento Bee* reporter Carlos Alcala said, "They stopped speaking to me. It was impossible to get any kind of explanation."[14]

Later, Garcia said, "We didn't comment on it because his contract wouldn't allow us to. We couldn't comment on any aspect of it. But he [Terry Grier] wasn't implementing our vision, like with the financing of the school district building."[15]

Citizens who had been following the controversy were shocked at the dismissal. CPEE often disagreed with Grier, but pushed to keep him as superintendent. It seemed, the firing had more to do with politics than anything else: a letter from Russell and Price to Grier, criticizing him for making disparaging comments about board members and creating dissent among Latinos and African Americans, was leaked to the press.[16] The board bought out his contract for just under $200,000.

---

[13]Maureen Fitzgerald.

[14]Carlos Alcala, telephone interview, April 17, 2000.

[15]Gaspar Garcia.

[16]Carlos Alcala, "School Board May Try to Oust Grier Today, Member Says," *Sacramento Bee*, November 7, 1995.

RECALL!

The closed-door firing of Grier and the refusal to explain why instantly inspired a recall effort against the "Gang of Four." A rally was held the Saturday after the firing and a storefront headquarters was set up behind a Burger King off Florin Road. It was led by Sam Walton, an African-American parent of students in the district.

"There were teachers, political organizers, and recognizable types like City Councilman Sam Pannell present," wrote Diana Griego Erwin, "but most of those attending were just normal folks, parents—mad parents, fed-up parents, parents saying, 'That's it! Something must be done.'"[17]

In the aftermath of the report and the firing, it seemed certain that the make-up of the board would change. Even the three other board members—Wimberly, Masoner, and Griffin—joined the effort against their colleagues. The mayor was ambivalent about a recall, which he felt should be used only as a tool against corruption. He would not support it, and, instead, asked all the board members to step down. None of the seven would agree. Serna and the four targets of the recall traded arguments in public and private. Garcia was especially angry, "He called me in Long Beach and told me to resign. I told him to go to hell. The people elected me just as they elected him. They wanted to get rid of the minorities on the board. They got the power structure to back the recall. The white people on the board were just as much to blame. Why didn't they try to recall them?"[18]

Proponents failed to get enough signatures to qualify for the March 1996 ballot. But 20,000 signatures in less than 30 days reflected the growing dissatisfaction with city schools. Meanwhile, ousted superintendent Terry Grier sued the district, accusing the board of violating the Brown Act by not allowing for proper notification of dismissal.

COUNSELING A DYSFUNCTIONAL FAMILY

In November 1994, the board began to search for a new superintendent. Jim Sweeney, who had been brought in as deputy superintendent under Grier,

---

[17] "If Opposition Jells, Trustees Should Leave," *Sacramento Bee*, November 19, 1995.
[18] Gaspar Garcia.

served as interim superintendent. Almost immediately, there was contro-versy. On a list of finalists was Gaspar Garcia's good friend from his days at University of Southern California, the superintendent of the Centinela Valley Union High School District. Joe Carrillo had a reputation for engendering controversy. He had applied for an administrative position in Sacramento in 1995, which he did not receive. The board minority was convinced another 4-3 vote would make him another hasty hire in the list of revolving door superintendents. Ted Kimbrough, former superintendent in Chicago and Compton, was brought in as an interim superintendent.

In the midst of making personnel decisions, the school board took a break in March and convened for a $1,450 "therapy session" at the Clarion hotel. A mediator was called in to teach them how to work as a team; the third time the board had tried such an intervention. The session did not seem to help. A new interim superintendent was chosen in a closed meeting, convened with little public notice, in May 1996. In a 4-3 vote, after three of the four members in the majority had lost their bid for reelection, the board approved a three-year contract with Ted Kimbrough. A quick decision was essential, the board explained because the majority was impressed with his work and the Los Angeles Unified School District was interested in hiring him.

Maureen Fitzgerald said she looked forward to working with Kimbrough but was concerned by the quick, secretive decision: "I don't think it's the way to bring our community along. This is an important decision. It should have been a much more public process."[19]

WHOSE ZOO?

In late May 1996, school board President Ida Russell proposed that the board create a commission to study conditions at the city zoo. It was a sarcastic response to the final report from the Mayor's Commission on Education and the City's Future, which recommended overturning of the school board. In June, the board voted to put a $225 million bond measure on the November ballot. While the four board members and the superinten-dent argued in favor of the measure, it received a lukewarm response from

---

[19]Deborah Anderluh, "Split Board Makes School Chief's Appointment Permanent," *Sacramento Bee*, May 8, 1996, A1.

community leaders who lacked confidence in the board and felt there would no chance to mobilize support in order to get the two-thirds majority necessary.

In July, 20 local business leaders announced a committee to fund and organize campaigns for four school board candidates. Serna distanced himself from the project as cochairs, Phil Angelides and Jon Kelly, of KCRA-TV, began interviewing candidates in August. "It was at the Money Store," recalled candidate Jay Schenirer. "It was a very crowded room with 15-20 community leaders sitting around the table. I was sitting directly across from Phil Angelides and John Kelly; they asked a lot of questions. We knew that it was going to be very competitive."[20]

The slate was announced at the beginning of September. Schenirer, a former legislative analyst and restauranteur, was general manager of Sacramento Food Bank Services. Manny Hernandez, a former legislative aide, owned a private consulting firm. Karen Young was a parent activist. Rick Jennings II was executive director of St. Hope Academy. The committee made a conscious effort to back a diverse slate, and with one African-American man (Jennings), one Latino (Hernandez), one Caucasian man (Schenirer), and one Caucasian woman (Young), they began campaigning.

Gaspar Garcia and Louise Perez, running for re-election, were very critical of the slate. (Members Russell and Wimberly declined to seek another term.) Parent and community groups that pushed for more public accessibility also expressed concern. Maureen Fitzgerald recalled a sense that outsiders were picking the board: "People were real concerned. Who would [the slate] be accountable to? I heard a lot of people talk about that."[21] The SCTA endorsed two slate members, Jennings and Schenirer.

With 28 people in the race, the visibility gained by being a member of the slate was invaluable, especially in a race where incumbents have the advantage of name recognition. Manny Hernandez remembers about 10 community forums, some only modestly attended. Other forums had 200-300 people, and one drew 600 people. Said Hernandez, "You can imagine the level of engagement here. There were radio interviews, the public channel did some interviews, did some debating. It was rather rigorous. It was like

---

[20]Jay Schenirer.
[21]Maureen Fitzgerald.

running in a mayor's race or something. And the *Sac Bee* covered it extensively."[22] Concern about the condition of the schools and a sense of crisis had taken hold in Sacramento.

In November 1996, the slate, with endorsements and financial backing from the business community, the support of the mayor, and cautious support from community members anxious for change, swept the school board election. The slate joined sitting members Michelle Masoner, Tom Griffin, and Virgil Price.

NEW BOARD, SAME OLD PROBLEM

When the new Sacramento School Board met for the first time in December 1996, the biggest change seemed to be in its attitude. The bickering of the old board was gone, replaced by an effort to create more accessibility and accountability through community outreach. They revised financial decisions, agreed to televise board meetings, and discussed management style. Masoner and Griffin always sided with the slate; Price often sided against the six board members.

What was the mayor's role? Jay Schenirer recalled a conversation they had the day after the election:

He said to me, 'This is now your deal. Let me know what you need.' He would hold us accountable for results . . . which I think is totally appropriate. But he had no desire nor did he ever get involved in running the district . . . he became the role model of how a mayor should be involved. He was helpful in our bond elections and supportive of whatever we needed.

Having stretched the boundaries, Serna stepped away.

After the election of the slate, charges of racism plagued the new board and the new administration. It began, according to Schenirer, with the board's decision to buy out Superintendent Ted Kimbrough's contract. Kimbrough, an African American, had supporters in the community who felt there might be ulterior motives to the board's decision other than differences in management styles. Others criticized the fact that the buy-out cost the district roughly $200,000. The charges of racism may have had roots in the

---

[22]Manny Hernandez, personal interview, March 10, 2000.

recall campaign in 1995. To this day, Garcia maintains the impetus was resentment against a board dominated by people of color.[23]

The selection of Jim Sweeney as interim superintendent, and the administrative changes that followed, referred to as the "May Massacre," led to fresh charges of racial bias, culminating in a dozen lawsuits. Sweeney was adamant that the lawsuits were frivolous, and he would ask the courts to make those who brought the charges pay the district's legal fees. Exasperated, he said, "I had a guy file a lawsuit which he later withdrew who claimed that he was being discriminated against because he was white, male, and over 45. We had other people sue us because they were black, female, and under 45. I mean, give us a break! You're white, male, and over 45? So am I."[24]

Despite the lawsuits and allegations that they are puppets of the mayor or the business community, the board members put students first. They have actively sought public-private partnerships and initiated a district-wide reading program, Open Court, in elementary schools with the help of the Packard Humanities Institute. A $195 million bond measure was approved by nearly 4/5 of those voting. In the "Taj Mahal," the district's literacy mission is plastered on the walls, along with motivational messages and bright, colorful pictures, contrasting sharply with the gray walls of the administrative building.

Garcia says it is easier to be successful with money, and while he sat on the board a recession drastically reduced district funds. He remains critical of Serna, and charges that the mayor ultimately harmed public education by getting involved. Garcia contends that the bickering of the old board was not political—simply the result of different people expressing the diverse views they were elected to represent. School board members Hernandez and Schenirer, and Superintendent Sweeney say that Serna never wanted to run the school board. Once the slate was elected, he simply stepped back and let the board make its decisions.

---

[23]Gaspar Garcia.

[24]Jim Sweeney, personal interview, March 14, 2000.

Case 8

INTRODUCTION

This case was *For the Birds*—not pejoratively of course—and the author provides a generous description of the South Spit. Was this for decorative, color purposes? Or, did the spit itself play a role in forcing and shaping a solution?

The problem depicted seemed like a no-win situation for so long that political inertia set in. Why else would super-aggressive entrepreneurial interests, cause-motivated activists, and a hyper-offended local populace fail to act for so long? What finally precipitated the risk-taking involved? Can you identify fully the key actors and the risks they faced?

Who were the public officials involved and why did it take them so long to act? Which ones were inclined to act cooperatively rather than evade responsibility? Why were they able and willing to act? What special insights, experience, attributes, or status did they possess?

This is a case where authority is fragmented. The solution would not have worked without the cooperation of various levels of government; policy-makers and bureaucrats; public officials and private citizens. Was it a "stick or carrot" that finally did the job? How successful was mediation? How much of a role did budget action play? How was a public health finding converted into a powerful political weapon? Was the ostensible discovery of a contagious disease an act of leadership or manipulation? If you were to conclude it was the latter, did the end justify the means?

This case highlights the extraordinary role of exceptional staff. Was the delegation of authority by a state senator to a field staff person appropriate? Why did he have such stunning confidence in her? What special faculties did she possess?

If you had been faced with the problem, what actions might you have taken? Were there key circumstances without which a good outcome was unlikely? Can you imagine a more successful scenario than that which emerged? If not, upon which of the key actors would you place leadership medals, and why?

111

Creative Collaboration: Regaining the South Spit—For the Birds

Research and original writing by Senate Fellow Megan Walseth

SPIT IN THE WIND

In Humboldt County, beaches matter. Whale watchers and anglers, surf riders and four-wheelers, bird counters and bird hunters—nature lovers of every stripe—battle for access, making the county's *Dunes Management Plan* its most important and contentious document. How, then, was a five-mile stretch of the North Coast's most spectacular shoreline collectively ignored and buried under heaps of garbage for years? How could a community so protective of its natural environment let hundreds of tons of trash sully this strip while its timber industry withered and tourism exploded? Surely, the trash belonged to someone.

Depending on the time of year, between one and three hundred people lived on the South Spit. People society might consider homeless called the spit home. Dominating the spit, their scruffy encampments lacked infrastructure, garbage removal or sewers, and were devoid of running water and electricity. Humboldt residents complained about lost recreation, condemned the raw sewage, anguished over the barefoot children, feared the dog packs, and resented the hostile faces of some residents. Yet, there was no great uprising, no widespread demand to run out the campers. Even formal organizations that had vigorously contested the Dunes Management Plan remained mostly silent. The people of the spit—people, like themselves—were an eyesore; that was certain. But since when had survival become a crime? And against whom? Who owned the land anyway? Of whom could anyone demand their ouster?

The answer was enveloped in fog as thick as the gray shroud that often cloaked the spit itself. Significant portions of the spit's land had simply accreted. Added by natural events—wind, weather, currents—since the land

113

had last been surveyed, they were of uncertain ownership. Enforcement of property rights would not be easy. Yet, surely, the greatest good for the greatest number would justify, even dictate, removal of the South Spit's permanent population. Jobs from tourism and recreation depended upon it. Protecting the land, water, and wildlife depended upon it. So did a public sense of well-being; even, perhaps, the public health.

As repository of the duty to protect health and safety, Humboldt County was asked to take action. Rather predictably, it joined with the spit's principal owner in an attempt to evict the campers. On the books, the county contemplated, unhappily, a strategy that would require years of litigation and immense legal resources. Off the books, officials feared accusations of discrimination and mean-spiritedness. They could get whipsawed (a phrase well understood in timber country) between friends of the homeless on the left and antigovernment sentiment on the right.

"You can't wade in and duke it out in the Attorney General's office," said County Harbor District Commissioner Jimmy Smith.[1] In order to convince Humboldt residents to accept any forced exodus of the campers, he said, "You need a network of people who communicate and understand the issues."

THE RISE OF PERMANENT ENCAMPMENTS

To the visitor driving north on U.S. 101, past Scotia and Fortuna, Humboldt Bay appears suddenly out the driver-side windows. Beyond the lush grazing land of seemingly ancient dairy farms, a calm green bay shows itself. Against the blue horizon of ocean and sky, one can just see the South Spit, a thin gray line separating Humboldt Bay from a feisty, occasionally terrifying, Pacific Ocean. Hence, the jetty—a stone and concrete seawall constructed in the 1960s by the U.S. Corps of Engineers. There, after jutting out of Table Bluff and running five narrow miles due north, the spit ends. The jetty itself turns abruptly westward, at a right angle extending into the ocean where, with its sibling on the North Spit, it protects vessels entering the bay.

---

[1] All quotations attributed to Jimmy Smith are from an interview conducted February 12, 1998, at Ramone's Café in downtown Eureka, California.

The North Spit, which boasts the incorporated town of Samoa and a Louisiana-Pacific pulp mill, is much wider than the South Spit. It is connected by a bridge to the city of Eureka. South Spit is narrow and difficult to access. For years, the 15-mile trip from Eureka—south to the town of Loleta at the south end of the bay, up the winding road to Table Bluff, and down steeply to the spit—kept it a treasure known only to Humboldt's locals. They came to fish and shoot ducks and play in the sand. "You can imagine how appealing this place was, how much use it got over the years," says one Eureka resident, her voice trailing off as she remembers what it became.[2]

In the mid-1980's, the U.S. Fish and Wildlife Service began to purchase land around the eastern perimeter of the bay, creating the Humboldt Bay National Wildlife Refuge. The refuge put the nearby South Spit on the tourist's map. Increased familiarity with the surrounding land brought more recreational use—including camping—to the South Spit (often referred to by campers as the "South Jetty," though jetty technically denotes the structure at the end of the spit). In increasing numbers, folks would pull their RVs and campers down to the spit for a few weeks of summertime fishing, an activity quite familiar to any Humboldt County resident.

In the late 1980s, the camping population began to change. People stayed longer; camps became more permanent; many visitors had no other homes. Humboldt County Supervisor Stan Dixon notes that the change coincided with California's recession: Californians were poor and counties, with deteriorating budgets, could do little to help.[3]

The South Jetty became an alternative haven. Shepherding the homeless off doorsteps and out of parks, Eureka police would commonly tell them to go to the South Jetty, where they wouldn't be bothered. Though officially denied by the Eureka Police Department, county officials corroborate stories like Larry's: "I was sleeping in my car and [the police] said I couldn't do that," the jetty resident told a Humboldt County reporter. "I asked where I could go, and they said 'the South Jetty'."

---

[2]All quotations attributed to Liz Murguia are from interviews conducted between February 11 and February 13, 1998.

[3]All quotations attributed to Stan Dixon are from an interview conducted on February 11, 1998, at the Humboldt County courthouse in Eureka

In any case, the county's homelessness problem was real. One could argue—and some did—that both Eureka and the county were unresponsive. There was no permanent shelter for the homeless, and monthly rents were near impossible for people on public assistance. A draft housing element released by the city of Eureka showed a shortage of some 966 low-income housing units. One homeless advocate wrote that "until the $226 County General Relief grant is raised to afford its recipients enough money to pay their monthly rental obligation," jetty residents would have few other choices.[4] The city of Eureka, said some, wanted only to move the homeless on. ("If a man's homeless, what is he gonna do? Walk around his whole life? And you can't go mission to mission either.")

ON THE JETTY: A PROBLEM TO WHOM?

So on they went—to the South Jetty. Campers nestled into subtle alcoves all along the spit, backs to the ocean, faces to the relative calm of the bay. Their dwellings were improvised; few of the tents, vans, trucks, buses, and campers they inhabited would have met the requirements of other mobile home or RV parks. The more community-oriented settled near the north end of the spit, clustering around what came to be known as "the Plaza." The Plaza was a grouping of settlements on a wide, flat area created by the Corps of Engineers as the staging ground for construction of the jetty. This widest section of the spit—not more than three city blocks—included a playground for children, a church built by North Coast Love in Action, which provided Sunday religious services, and a weekly food bank. Linda Clough, a 41-year-old mother of two and five-year spit resident, came to the spit when her house "back East" was destroyed by fire. "There's all these sanctuaries for animals and there's nothing for humans," she said. Susan Dunn, mother and grandmother to 13—many of whom were with her on the spit—told a reporter that she "came to the spit recently to escape a man who had been stalking her and her family." Five-year resident Michael Allen Highland describes how he "used to work for the timber company," but was injured on

---

[4]Sara Senger, "'Emergency on Jetty a False Alarm'" (press release), September 25, 1997.

the job. "My legs are history," he said.[5] Social services worker Ernest Ingraham knows their stories: "This is the height of misery," he said. "These are the poorest of the poor. They have nowhere else to go."[6]

Some people overcame drug and alcohol problems on the jetty, and found a place that felt like home. These stories of hardship and poverty were familiar to the families of those Humboldt County residents who worked in the woods, in the mills, in the factories, and on the docks. A significant percentage of them, says Mark Wheetley of the California Coastal Conservancy, "can identify with being on that economic fringe. They know it could be them."[7]

The community on the jetty, like most communities, was diverse, and other stories may have been less sympathetic. "I've never been homeless," said Lurch, who lived on the jetty for seven years.[8] He and others like him say they are not meant for life in town, that they sleep easier under the stars. Some jetty families, says Loleta School Superintendent Jim Malloy, "didn't want a permanent house . . . . [They] had the opportunity to live in a more permanent setting, but they chose this. . . . [Some said they had a] monthly income—and it's a tax free monthly income—of $1,250 . . . in addition to [public assistance.]"[9]

If the life was a choice for some of the adults, it certainly was not for the spit's children. This was troublesome to many observers of the situation. It is difficult to say with precision how many children lived on the spit. Most estimates put the number between 35 and 50, though Malloy notes that this number—and charges of their lack of supervision—were often exaggerated by those favoring eviction. Malloy, who on his first days as superintendent three years ago went down to the jetty to discuss obstacles to attendance in a positive manner, said that the jetty kids' attendance was equal to that of the

---

[5]Kie Relyea, "Testing the Constitution: Community on the South Spit," *Times-Standard* (Eureka), October 5, 1997.

[6]Nancy Brands Ward, "Emotions Mixed During Relocation," *Humboldt Beacon,* October 23, 1997.

[7]All quotations attributed to Mark Wheetley are from interviews conducted on February 13, 1998, at the South Spit and at the Waterfront Café in downtown Eureka, California.

[8]Nancy Brands Ward.

[9]All quotations attributed to Jim Malloy are from an interview conducted on February 12, 1998, at the Loleta School in Loleta, California.

other students. Still, observers wondered whether society should support this style of living, especially when what they thought they saw were children unsupervised and poorly clothed, playing among "a mountain of refrigerators . . . raw sewage in buckets . . . eight Honda Civics,"[10] or in another's words, "excrement, garbage, discarded drug paraphernalia and abandoned and burned vehicles."[11]

Few dispute that the jetty appeared a "Third World" environment and a "horrible eyesore," but jetty residents rightly protested that the garbage problem was not entirely their own.[12] "I saw a contractor come out here with a pickup full of [dry wall] and garbage," said a jetty resident named Betty. "He dumped it and took off. We got blamed." Leonard, whose old school bus was reportedly one of the cleaner camps, pointed out that there are no sanitation facilities for weekend visitors: "So people show up and see toilet paper in the bushes and they look at us."[13] Source aside, the junk and human waste were a strain upon the sensitive coastal ecosystem. Seabirds who used to stop in their migrations were scared off—some said by the packs of dogs and livestock belonging to jetty campers. Jimmy Smith, now a commissioner of the Humboldt Harbor, Recreation, and Conservation District, monitored waterbirds daily. "Migrating shorebirds," he says, "are not compatible with dogs, feral cats, and livestock." The nature lovers of Humboldt County felt equally incompatible: "You really felt for [some of the people]," said one such person. But overall, "the feeling was very intimidating. . . . Everybody had drugs, everybody had guns, everybody had dogs. Well, just about everybody."[14]

And it was true that, as much as a haven for the down-and-out, the South Jetty was a magnet for the lawless—the "heathens,"[15] as one long-term, community-oriented jetty resident called them. Several bodies turned up on the spit. Meth labs, and the guns they brought with them, were not uncom-

---

[10]Mark Wheetley.

[11]Kie Relyea, "Campers' Ouster Sought," *Times-Standard* (Eureka), March 26, 1994. Quoting Loleta Volunteer Fire Dept. Chief David Fidjeland.

[12]And homeless advocates point out that the situation was probably a great deal safer than that of the homeless in America's cities.

[13]Patrick Mullins, "The Other Side: South Jetty Residents Say They're Misunderstood," *Humboldt Beacon*, May 12, 1994.

[14]Mark Wheetley.

[15]Patrick Mullins.

mon. Several social workers were shot at. "It is widely known through Northern California that if you want to get away with anything, do it on the South Spit of Humboldt Bay," said David Fidjeland, chief of the volunteer fire department in the neighboring town of Loleta. It was he and his fellow volunteers who, fed up with responding to calls from the spit (which "contributed little to our tax base" yet made up 20 percent of the department's calls) began to collect the critical mass necessary to advocate for change. Chief Fidjeland came to Humboldt County Supervisor Stan Dixon for help. "Out of sight and out of mind" for the rest of the county, said Fidjeland, residents of Loleta could not continue to put up with the encampment.[16] (Other Loleta residents planted a seed with State Senator Mike Thompson, telling him of their distaste for the campers at a Fortuna town hall meeting. It would be ever after on his radar screen, and more importantly, on that of his district staffer, Liz Murguia, whom he told to fix it. She got on the phone with Mark Wheetley.)

OWNERSHIP: "THIS LAND IS YOUR LAND"

The county's first step was to determine ownership. Supervisor Dixon contacted his friend Mark Wheetley, a one-time Humboldt State University resource management student now employed in his dream job with the Coastal Conservancy—a state entity that sponsors local projects for coastal restoration and recreation. He began an official study of the ownership and ecology of the South Spit. The Pacific Lumber Company was the principal owner with some 660 acres. With Wheetley's help, the county determined that parts of the remainder were owned by various federal entities, as might be the "accreted land"—land built up by construction and natural processes that did not exist at the time the titles were drawn up. Texaco was said to own some, as well as other private owners. The county owned a parcel. But none of this determined official legal ownership or designated boundaries, and the official machinations of private property would prove too confusing to be of much use. (Having completed the initial survey, Wheetley started on a management plan, approaching various agencies and asking whether they would be interested in management or acquisition. Liz, Stan, Jimmy, and

---

[16]Kie Relyea.

Mark would put their heads together frequently, informally, imagining who might buy it and how.)

The Pacific Lumber Company, whose majority ownership was obvious if the exact boundaries of its parcel were not, was loath to alienate anyone by enforcing camping rules. As a company, "They had always been people-friendly," says Jimmy Smith, but had received "a lot of bad press" following their takeover by the Maxxam Corporation under Charles Hurwitz (of Headwaters controversy; his critics would say infamy). "Pacific Lumber," says Smith, "was reluctant to get involved." And the campers reminded them that they would not go gently: Together with Humboldt County, which owned another relatively clear parcel of land on the south end of the spit, the company erected a sign detailing camping rules and restrictions. The sign was "torn down, burned down, shot down" in a matter of days, says Wheetley.

Pacific Lumber was not alone in its reluctance to address the people problem. The U.S. Fish and Wildlife Service, which had at one time been interested in adding the South Spit to its wildlife preserve, had backed off when it became apparent that the residents were there to stay. Part of this reluctance came from the possibility of falling out of favor with the local community by causing additional hardship for the spit residents—a perfect story for the local papers. Even greater reluctance stemmed from the very real and costly legal issue of prescriptive rights, which are those an individual develops by using private property for five years or more without the owner's consent. One who has developed prescriptive rights cannot be evicted unless provided for under the Relocation Act, which guarantees the evictee General Relief plus 48 months of standard, safe housing.

The Jettites, generally not advocates for the protection of property rights, nonetheless used its red tape to their advantage. Because there were so many owners, campers could easily move around, not camping on private land when restrictions were being enforced more rigorously. Generally, they moved to the Plaza, which—if in fact owned by the federal government—was not regulated as if it were.

WORLD VS. JETTITES:
ROUND ONE, "THIS LAND IS MY LAND"

During 1993, Pacific Lumber began evicting Jettites from its property according to the usual legal process. The county sheriff served eviction notices to some fifteen individuals, and their cases were heard in court. Not only was this a drop in the bucket—15 people compared with the entire population—but the campers could simply move to the Plaza. Court-appointed counsel for the cases cost the county over $100,000, money it could ill afford. Counsel advised Supervisor Dixon that a wider lawsuit would be necessary, that the individual eviction process would not accomplish the clearing of the spit.

Humboldt County, lacking resources, joined with Pacific Lumber and the Loleta Volunteer Fire Department to file a lawsuit in late March of 1994. Citing health, safety, and zoning violations, it called for the campers to vacate the area, which would then be closed while the various owners came up with a plan for management of the land. This approach, however, soon appeared to be as doomed as was eviction. The defendants, represented by Jan Turner of Redwood Legal Assistance, argued that there had been an "implied public dedication of the property." Turner and her colleagues would do whatever they could to find a way for the campers to stay on the jetty, charging that the county could easily provide food and water. "They went to the extreme very quickly," says Wheetley, who believes that the advocates made a mistake in focusing their energy on trying to accommodate the campers on the spit rather than on looking for another place. "It was a confrontation," says Jim Malloy. "I don't believe there was any time in which people sat down and said, 'These are our concerns.' It was, 'How do we move them off?'"

The plaintiffs eventually conceded that "litigation over titles would be very expensive and time consuming."[17] Given the specter of relocation costs and the determination of the defendants, Dixon realized that the suit could become a bottomless pit of legal expenses, and proposed that the parties begin a formal mediation process. With professional mediators from Humboldt State University, the parties agreed that "public and private funds could be more responsibly used" to develop a compromise.

This allowed homeless advocates to broaden the issue, using the situation of the South Jetty as a way to confront general homelessness issues. Advocates wanted to protect the campers' community lifestyle. In mediation, they could continue to demand that the county provide services for those

---

[17]Superior Court of California, County of Humboldt. Stipulated Judgment and Order. Case No. 94DROO80. (Settlement).

living on the jetty, but they could also push for an alternative location that would accommodate the community—at county expense. During simultaneous housing element negotiations they pushed for a county nomadic park which, says Dixon, would have had very few rules or restrictions. "The real problem," said Turner, "is that the public doesn't care about the homeless and the government doesn't want to deal with the problem."[18]

"Some select groups," says Jimmy Smith, referring, presumably, to people like Turner, "were in favor of a wider treatment of the homeless problem." To some extent, they succeeded. Wheetley says the South Spit drama did kickstart a multi-agency effort to deal with homelessness. "We met twice a week, like it was an emergency." When the issue came to be one of homelessness generally, many environmental groups—whose members were presumably sympathetic to this similarly progressive, if not complementary cause—refused to take a position, refused to step forward. "I was disappointed in the environmental community," says Wheetley. "They could have done a lot more." Wheetley felt that nine out of 10 community members probably favored clearing the spit, but the inertia was powerful.

STRATEGY SHIFT:
SAVE THE DUCKS! (LOSE THE PEOPLE)

Wheetley's management activities had begun at roughly the same time as the efforts to evict the residents. Looking past eviction, determined to be ready should it occur, Wheetley met with scores of agencies, floating the possibility of purchase and management, to develop the plan. Almost all were very hands off, says Jimmy Smith. Yet without some assurance of acquisition or some resolution after eviction, says Wheetley, the county "never had the gumption to go forward." The county simply hadn't the resources to take on the responsibility of management, which would require much more than just acquisition. To ensure that the spit maintained the desired character, it would be necessary to construct restrooms, to improve the road, and to provide staff for enforcement of controlled access and general maintenance.

By reputation, Senator Thompson does not accept inertia. In late November 1993, Thompson—an avid duck hunter—had toured this once-

---

[18]Dan Udseth, "Life on the Jetty May Change," *Humboldt Beacon*, June 26, 1996.

prime, now environmentally degraded hunting ground. At a town hall meeting in Fortuna soon after, Thompson said: "I was out there, and I am troubled by it. [Some of] the folks who are out there [don't] want to work, at least that's my observation . . . . There is a real problem out there."[19]

LIZ

Senator Thompson told his staff, chiefly veteran Field Representative and longtime Humboldt resident Liz Murguia, to do something about it. With his backing, Murguia, born and raised on the North Coast—the granddaughter, daughter, sister, and mother of loggers—worked with Wheetley on the management plan.

In June 1996, Thompson took action. Despite continued ambivalence from other agencies and groups, he introduced SB 39, which would authorize the Wildlife Conservation Board and the Coastal Conservancy to acquire the spit, using available funds. SB 39 would provide $100,000 for acquisition and planning; an Assembly appropriations committee analysis estimated the purchase cost of the spit to be between $500,000 and $1,000,000. In order to pass the legislature, the bill was amended to require that the South Spit be cleared "of any illegal encampment, debris, and other environmental hazards by the current property owner" before the plan was enacted or the land acquired by the state. Thompson attempted to help the South spit process through his position as chair of the Senate Budget Committee. Governor Pete Wilson, however, twice deleted budget augmentations—in the 1996 Budget Act, $100,000 from the Coastal Conservancy for acquisition, and in the 1997 Budget Act, $160,000 from the Department of Fish Game for management and maintenance costs. The governor argued that management of the land was a local responsibility, at least until it became state property. In an unusual alignment, the governor found himself the recipient of hearty congratulations from Ruben Botello of the American Homeless Society, and of criticism from the conservative Eureka *Times-Standard*, which does not normally support public acquisitions.

Despite the governor's actions, there was still no way to force the campers off and SB 39 funds—as well as the interest of possible buy-

---

[19]Glenn Franco Simmons, "Thompson Cites South Jetty 'Mess'," *Humboldt Beacon*, November 18, 1993.

ers—were dependent upon clearing the spit of campers. The bill did increase media coverage of the issue, and begin to shift the tone of the mediation process. According to Stan Dixon, the bill made all involved realize that ultimately, the Jettites would be relocated. In giving Wheetley's management plan an official format, the bill gave the county the "gumption" to go forward. "Mike's bill really put the pressure on," says Jimmy Smith. Management of the spit was "beyond [the county's] capacity. It solidified their position" to know that someone would buy the land, that the process was in motion. Jim Malloy felt this was a step in the right direction, an approach which asked "not so much 'How do you move the people off?' but instead, 'How do you handle this natural resource.?' This was a more productive view. It led to progress."

The mediation efforts were nearing completion, but mediation involves compromise. Concessions by the county would allow campers to remain on designated portions of the spit. Humboldt County would provide intensive case management to those who wanted it, but could not prevent them from returning to the South Spit. The county could not, under the terms of the agreement, interfere with camping in designated areas unless laws had been broken ("for acts which threaten other users or the public, including discharge of fecal matter on the ground, dumping, littering, etc."). In today's workfare climate, the concessions gained by homeless advocates seem substantial: Employable residents remaining on the spit would not be subject to work-for-relief requirements unless they had working vehicles with which they could reach their work assignments within 40 minutes, or unless the county provided transportation, or sited the assignment within two miles of the remote spit. The county promised to make its housing element a priority, and would improve the South Spit road and arrange for garbage service and toilets. Should the county acquire the area, it agreed not to seek the community's ouster until a "reasonable" alternative was purchased, as defined.[20]

Still, the county didn't have the resources to acquire the area, and SB 39 funds depended on a clean, unpopulated South Spit. In August 1997, when the settlement was finished and signatures were being gathered, those involved in the management plan realized that an uninhabited spit was still a long way off. "We thought it would be several years" before the management plan could be enacted," says Wheetley. "We kept imagining what the

---

[20]Superior Court.

scenarios would be for [clearing the spit of its inhabitants]," remembers Liz Murguia. "Then Ann Lindsay came in—that was our saving [grace]."

"ANN LINDSAY'S *GESTAPO TACTICS*"

On September 2, 1997, Dr. Ann Lindsay, Humboldt County's Public Health Officer, declared an outbreak of shigella (bacterial diarrhea) and ordered the evacuation of the spit within 30 days. The community was stunned. "They'll have to shoot me," said Merle Adams. "I ain't got nowhere to go. I don't want to die, but I'd die in the town anyway. I can't get along with people in town."[21] Indeed, this had been a uniting factor for the Jettites all along—a feeling that Eurekans were hostile toward them, a feeling that doors slammed in their faces. "We, the people of the South Jetty, are being discriminated against in a manner similar to Hitler's Germany. If we are so ill, why hasn't the Health Department offered us some medical aid such as antibiotics," wrote Michele Monterrey in a letter to the Eureka *Times-Standard*.[22] A "South Jetty Love March for the Homeless" was organized. "The level of stress, fear, and general anxiety is rising markedly among jetty residents," reported Nancy Dervin, director of North Coast Love in Action, a religious group that had provided services on the jetty. "What the county is doing to these people is heartless and cruel."[23]

Public outcry over the order was intense, but brief and concentrated. Dervin called the action a "hostile takeover by the local government," arguing that there had "been no verifiable cases of shigella or any other disease for over two months." She stated that the $55,000 initially requested of the county by Dr. Lindsay could have provided water, toilets, and garbage service for two-and-a-half years.[24] Jan Turner asked, "Has an emergency on the South Spit arisen since the county signed the agreement on August 19, 1997, or is this a pretext to achieve a political goal the county has been unable to accomplish through the courts?" She warned other county residents to pay attention: "If you permit your government to deprive the

---

[21]Rhonda Parker, "Some Refuse to Leave Spit," *Times-Standard* (Eureka), October 21, 1997.

[22]October 21, 1997.

[23]Nancy Dervin, "Fact Sheet" and "Declaration,"September 23, 1997.

[24]*Ibid.*

homeless of their constitutional rights, it can take away your rights as well," read a news statement issued by her organization.[25] Although Dr. Lindsay confirmed that "there have been no cases of Shigella reported since August 12th," she argued that "the conditions that caused the outbreak of this infectious condition still exist and can only be addressed by moving the 300 campers off the jetty."[26]

The timing of the order was certainly suspicious. How could Dr. Lindsay not have known how badly this was needed, especially now that the management plan was finally coming together? Did she act independently, without prompting from other county officials? Of course, says Stan Dixon, impervious to the perfect timing. He calls the action courageous, and though his relief is plain, nothing in his face or manner so much as recognizes the idea that such coincidence would appear more than lucky for the South Spit negotiators. For Smith, the declaration boils down to the fact that there was "finally a preponderance of evidence. [We were] an inch away from a health disaster even before the declaration." Smith's set was happy to accept Dr. Lindsay's rationale, and so, they think, were most residents of Humboldt County. Yet Jim Malloy of the Loleta School is responsive to the idea that other factors may have influenced the timing of the order. The county, he said, didn't want to do anything while the presence of meth labs on the spit raised the possibility of violence. After several social service workers were shot at, a "general memo came out [saying one] shouldn't go out to the jetty. If there was a meth lab out there, you could get shot at, but eventually the meth labs moved off. . . . [It] seemed to me that as long as the meth labs moved off, things got to moving. The county didn't want to put anyone in danger."

Jan Turner of Redwood Legal Assistance immediately filed a motion requesting that the county be forced to comply with the terms of the court settlement. A Superior Court Judge granted a temporary restraining order during review of the case, but ultimately ruled that the interest of public health was preeminent. The judge agreed that, as an official of the county, Dr. Lindsay may have been bound by the agreement. He argued, however, that she also had duties toward the state, and that the county's health

---

[25]Redwood Legal Assistance, press release, September 25, 1997.

[26]Ann Lindsay, M.D., "South Jetty Assistance Plan," *Public Health Notes*, July-September 1997.

authority was preeminent.[27] Supervisor Dixon adds that the agreement allowed for county action in emergency situations anyway, and notes that neither the Harbor District nor some of Jan Turner's clients had signed yet. "She's probably wishing she hadn't [stalled in getting those signatures]," says Dixon. Dr. Lindsay gave the Jettites 72 hours after the lifting of the restraining order to leave the spit.

LEAVING THE SPIT

The gains made by the homeless community, however paltry, were immediately washed away. At the time of the order, a gate had been erected at the entrance to the spit. Round the clock security guards ensured that access to the spit would be limited to its present occupants, 160 of whom (says Nancy Dervin) were given identification cards or bracelets allowing them to come and go until the deadline. "That was one intense little location," said Wheetley of the gated entrance. jetty campers were given vouchers for two free weeks at the Eureka Ranchotel, or two weeks free camping at a county park on the North Spit. Sixty-five vehicles were repaired, 139 tires were replaced, and many of the more stubborn home/vehicles were towed—at cost—by a local towing company. "We had a rat problem because of all the trash," says Wheetley, who remembers watching the rodents fall out the back of a camper being towed up Highway 101.

The campers would be intensively case managed according to a model developed at Columbia University called critical time intervention, in which assistance continues for up to six months after relocation. The assistance would be intensive, but fundamentally individual and oriented toward traditional housing. Homeless advocates had consistently opposed this approach in favor of accommodation at a group site, but Humboldt County's small army of social service workers nevertheless received high praise from all involved. "There are a lot of hard working, dedicated people out here working to carry out an inhumane plan," said Jan Turner.[28]

According to Jim Malloy, the relocation "worked really well for those families that wanted to be relocated." The families of students he tracked ended up in housing or in other homeless encampments, and the students are

---

[27]*Times-Standard* (Eureka), October 17 and 19, 1997.
[28]Nancy Brands Ward.

"all enrolled somewhere." He takes care in this statement, running through the names to himself, just to be sure: "Tony's mom? She has a place in Eureka." Stan Dixon admits that he wasn't sure that individual case management—as opposed to the mass resettlement advocated by the homeless organizations—would work. But after nearly four months, he believes that the success of the effort is "one of the strongest arguments against nomadic parks. If you actually deal with people on an individual basis, assistance is available." And perhaps not all was lost for homeless advocates. Increased attention to housing may have speeded along plans for a county multiple assistance center for the homeless. Still, said social services worker Ernest Ingraham at the time of the relocation, "We have not solved the homeless problem—we've just spread it around. Some of the cases are not resolvable."[29]

Once the campers were gone, the spit itself was cleaned. Peter Esko of the Department of Environmental Health estimates that 400 cubic yards of solid waste—50 dump trucks worth—had to be removed from the jetty, along with 110 abandoned vehicles and 400 tires. He estimated that 100 of the campsites contained household hazardous wastes.[30] The relocation and cleanup were funded by a state grant of some $140,000 from the Integrated Waste Management Board (IWMB). Humboldt County matched the grant—half with cash and half with in-kind services—and received almost $40,000 in private donations for relocation and cleanup. California Conservation Corps crews provided labor for the cleanup, and equipment was donated from all over the county. "Liz got the IWMB money," explains Mark Wheetley. On behalf of her boss, Murguia had drafted a letter to the IWMB asking it to look favorably on the grant to Humboldt County. ("It helped that Wesley [Chesboro, director of the IWMB,] was running for Mike's seat [in the state Senate]," says Murguia. "It was totally appropriate though," adds Wheetley. "They are going to hold it up as a model project for IWMB.")

---

[29]*Ibid.*

[30]Peter Esko, REHS, "Environmental Health to Oversee South Jetty Cleanup," *Public Health Notes*, July-September 1997.

THE FUTURE OF THE SPIT

Though the spit is still remote and will be difficult to manage, plans for a public park are moving along. The U.S. Fish and Wildlife Service (USFWS) has agreed to acquire the land, which will be purchased from the various entities and consolidated by Trust for Public Lands, then transferred to the USFWS and the Bureau of Land Management. The spit will be divided: the bay side will belong to the USFWS wildlife preserve, and the shore side will be for public recreation, including off-road vehicles.

In the interim, management problems have not evaporated. The homeless are not the only ones opposed to the current closure to vehicles. Fishermen argue that their livelihoods are dependent on coastal fishing. Waterfowl hunters will want their traditional access. Many in Humboldt County "are going to want to return to activities [they pursued] prior to the homeless occupation," says Jimmy Smith. He anticipates torturous public hearings in which one group will say, "It's our historical right . . . " and another will counter with, "Wait a second, you just kicked me out and now you're letting this group do that?"

"This is for the good of the order," Smith says of the current closure. "You can't discriminate between legitimate and illegitimate uses." Yet that appears to be what's happening. In response to criticism from people who say their livelihoods depend upon access to the spit, the county began issuing keys to the locked gate. "I'm special," says one man while unlocking the gated entrance to the spit. "It's day use for anyone, but most people have to walk. I'm here to salvage crab gear and firewood." Keys for day use will be distributed to anyone—anyone who knows whom to ask, that is. For his part, Mark Wheetley doubts that giving out the keys is "better than dealing with the voices" of those who want to use the South Spit.

There will always be controversy. Off-road vehicle riders will always fight environmentalists. Humboldt's fishermen will always demand their rights. But to Wheetley, what matters is that the South Spit is clean. The seabirds are returning, happily ignorant of the human drama that cleared their path. Wheetley is determined to maintain his vigilance, to see the project through to acquisition and successful management. He spends his evenings making presentations to groups like the Humboldt Coastal Coalition. He organizes a coastal cleanup day so that everyone can see the new spit and help with the restoration of native plants. If money falls short, he and Jimmy

Smith have gained the promise of some limited support from Senators Boxer and Feinstein in Washington.

Liz Murguia looks at the clean spit for the first time: "Partly it just makes you so mad that we had to beat people up to [be interested in acquiring the land.]" Murguia doesn't stay mad for long. Wheetley has come up with a new idea—that there should be a countywide special district for recreation and tourism. Instantly, the two are excited again, bouncing back to the idea throughout their conversation. With these two behind it, one suspects that it just might happen.

Case 9

INTRODUCTION

In a perfect world, public decisions proceed according to a plan designed to achieve a previously agreed upon public goal. In the real world, when public decisions do not proceed as planned, the blame is often attributed to *politics*. The argument takes many forms: Goals are set that benefit the powerful at the expense of the public. Science is abandoned in favor of pandering to radical causes. The self-interest of officials prevails over what they know to be ethically correct. Logic gives way to petty partisanship. Common sense citizens, the argument goes, would produce a better result than stupid public servants.

To whatever degree the criticisms hold water, they overlook a number of realities. First, attention is drawn to controversial decisions, not those where near-unanimity reigns and unremarkable transactions occur. When there is controversy, a system founded on democratic values seeks to placate, or at least reconcile diverse interests and objectives. In the process, public decision making often appear less efficient than it could be.

A controversial public decision may be far more complex than meets the eye. The media often report the predigested comments of patronizing officials. Fundamental uncertainties may exist just beneath that superficial understanding. Competing values may be deeply wedged between the symbols that serve to identify the opposing positions.

What happens when a pleasing confluence of energies produces a seemingly satisfactory result? Which, if any, of the apolitical virtues mentioned in the first paragraph is responsible? Is it luck? Or, could it actually be political leadership?

One characteristic of leadership may be the ability to recognize and programmatically synthesize opportunities that present themselves. Rather than a single identifiable leader focused on an end result, there may be a number of individuals, each seeking narrower objectives, who are drawn together by circumstances when the political stars are aligned. Absent a clearly sought outcome, how does one evaluate the results that are achieved?

Are they better or worse than what might have been achieved had conventional planning dominated?

Identify the various actors in *Boots to Birkenstocks* that were motivated by factors other than what ultimately resulted. What were their motives? Identify the circumstances that made the end result possible. Were there attractive alternatives competing for the land, and why did they lose out? What explanations provided a cover for those institutionally committed to an alternative planning and decision-making process? What circumstances brought those holding different federal, state, and local responsibilities into alignment? Could *extraordinary pressures* and *unique opportunities* justify virtually any political decision? Who were the winners and the losers among the affected constituencies? Would there be *a four-year university on the Monterey peninsula* without the politically inspired energies of the participants? Should there be *a four-year university on the Monterey peninsula?* Could the same resources have been amassed and applied in a better location?

Was the outcome, as Winston Churchill said of democracy, "the worst . . . except for all the others?"

Federalism Suspended: Boots To Birkenstocks

Research and original writing by Senate Fellow Owen M. Sweeney

BREAKING CAMP

California State University, Monterey Bay welcomed the first group of students through its gates, the gates of what had been Fort Ord, in September of 1995. Just four years earlier the U.S. Secretary of Defense announced that Fort Ord would be closed as a military base.[1] With the mass exodus of army personnel and civilian jobs, an extraordinary effort had been initiated to fill the economic void. Democrats and Republicans; federal, state, and local legislators; civilians and soldiers; private and public institutions; and community colleges and universities joined hands in a mighty, albeit odd, coalition. If you share the widely held opinion that public processes move at a snail's pace, note well that in less than 48 months a public university—CSU, Monterey Bay—was established. Combat boots were replaced with Birkenstocks.

PHOENIX RISING

When Fort Ord appeared on the Secretary of Defense's proposed base closure list in January of 1990, Monterey area Congressman Leon Panetta encouraged formation of a local task force to oppose the base closure—to no avail. When Fort Ord appeared on the final list of closures, Panetta and his 365-member task force accepted the decision and turned their attention to examining the needs of the surrounding region and constructing alternative uses for Fort Ord.

---

[1] It was on the list of base closures recommended by the Base Realignment and Closure Commission signed into existence by President Bush in November 1991.

A diverse cross-section of Monterey Bay area residents, the panel debated various proposals—theme parks, resort hotels, high-tech industrial parks, and, early on, a university.

The California State University system, however, was already in a bind. They were not only dealing with a recession-triggered budget reduction, and consequent limits on the ability of students to pay ever-increasing fees, but they were faced with a projected deluge of students. The so-called "Tidal Wave II," the second wave of sons and daughters of the baby-boomers, was about to wash up on CSU's steps.

Meanwhile, the federal government, in the post-Cold War process of closing its surplus military bases, was leaving economic black holes throughout the country, but particularly in California where a disproportionate number had been sited. With re-election on their minds, and perhaps more specifically California's large number of congressional seats and electoral votes, federal politicians desperately needed a "conversion showcase." It would help convince the public that vacated army bases could become sources of economic prosperity. According to CSU, MB's Vice President for Administration, Richard E. (Hank) Hendrickson, "They [Monterey region residents] had been wanting a four-year university here on this peninsula for probably forty years. . . ." It seemed a match made in heaven.

Hendrickson began his career with the CSU system as San Jose State's director of operations, design and construction after retiring as a full colonel from the U.S. Army. As the garrison commander of Fort Ord from 1985 until his retirement in 1989, he was the obvious choice to oversee the transformation. Hendrickson, along with vice president of San Jose State, J. Handel Evans (now planning president of CSU Channel Islands), was responsible for "getting the facility." After a July 1991 meeting between San Jose State officials and Panetta, Hendrickson was sent to his old base because he was acquainted with everybody who was still in command. His task, he says, was "to find out what we could do about getting maybe four or five buildings . . . to move our Salinas satellite center over here." While he approached the base officials with a modest request for a four or five building satellite center, he talked in his report to San Jose State about the possibilities of building *a four-year university* at Fort Ord. Chancellor Barry Munitz, and Trustees Anthony M. Vitti and William D. Campbell, encouraged Evans and Hendrickson to pursue the opportunity. By August of that year, continued development of other forces demonstrated to CSU the wisdom of pushing for a twenty-five thousand full-time-equivalent student university.

Evans then met with the local task force, chaired by Panetta, and pitched the full-time university proposal. "That became the issue that we deliberated on," he says, "and Leon and I had a conversation, and we both went to our own corners and worked on it, and the rest is history."

SELLING A CAMPUS

It is not every day that the federal government offers a university system two thousand acres of prime oceanfront property for free, plus the promise of $150 million to convert it into a viable campus. Said Campbell, "We didn't wake up one morning and decide that we had to have a campus at Fort Ord. The opportunity presented itself . . . and we faced a statewide demographic problem. It was terribly exciting."[2]

Tidal Wave II, the statewide demographic problem, provided a special impetus to CSU's rationale. Systemwide enrollments, then projected by the Demographic Research Unit in the Department of Finance, would increase to 399,375 full-time-equivalent students by 2010, an increase of approximately 140,000 students from 1992.[3] Those figures are now considered far overstated by sources such as California's Legislative Analyst and the Department of Finance. But at the time, Tidal Wave II was the brightest of what Evans' called his three "guiding lights" for the effort to obtain Fort Ord: "We knew that we had this enormous increase in enrollment coming down the pike in Tidal Wave II. We knew that this facility would give us an opportunity to have a university at less cost than building a new one in a place that we thought was a good place to have it. And we felt that with appropriate academic partnerships . . . we could do some very innovative work. We had this concept of bringing together existing educational institutions into one big partnership and to provide a different educational process for our students."[4]

---

[2]D. Campbell, telephone interview, February 1998.

[3]As quoted in the CPEC report 94-8, Breaking Camp—Building a Campus, 5, June 1994.

[4]Handel Evans, telephone interview, March 19, 1998.

This unforeseen gift, which could solve both the increased student demand and shortfall of funds, would also afford the State University system the ability to offer students what was touted to be *a new type of education,* focused on the use of technology while drawing upon the resources of the surrounding region. The new campus was to be the physical and cyber-nexus of existing educational facilities in the surrounding region, including several marine and agricultural research labs, the military's Defense Language Institute, the Naval Postgraduate School, and the Monterey International Studies Institute. It was to focus on innovation that transcended traditional educational practices. Rather than departments, the curriculum would be organized around academic clusters that would emphasize marine, atmospheric, and environmental science; the visual and performing arts; languages, cultures, and international studies; international business; and futuristic education. The new university was to be the prototypical *university of the next century.*

THE MASTER PLAN, CPEC AND CSU

A Master Plan for Higher Education in California, 1960-1975 was crafted during the late 1950s by a select and varied group of legislators and educators from state and local government and educational systems throughout California. The plan was an effort to depoliticize new campus placements after the overtly political placements of CSU Stanislaus and Sonoma State University. Former UC president and a guiding spirit of the Master Plan, Dr. Clark Kerr described the concerns of that time:

We in the University of California became nervous. Was the Legislature going to take over? We were particularly sensitive to Turlock (CSU Stanislaus) and Sonoma because in 1944 the state Legislature had given the University—not requested by it—the Santa Barbara State College, which later (after 1958) became a great asset to the University, but in 1944 it was imposed on the University. We were not anxious to see such intrusions by the Legislature into what we considered the internal affairs of higher education happen again. We were all very conscious then of our claimed autonomy. We were deeply concerned that the political process was taking over.[5]

William Chance of the now-defunct California Higher Education Policy Center wrote that the master plan was, "an implicit commitment . . . to a comprehensive decision-making process that would stress planning, explicitly identified criteria and priorities, and the inclusion of managerial oversight and statewide planning agencies to ensure that changes were monitored and decisions were justified by strong evidentiary need. . . . Analysis replaced politics, and priorities replaced boosterism."[6]

Said Pat Callan, head of the Higher Education Policy Institute and director of the California Postsecondary Education Commission from 1978 to 1986: "Politics will always be part of it when you're deciding where to put a campus. There's no question that is partly a political decision, but the concern was that if you let this become pork barrel politics so that what you end up with is a set of campuses whose location reflects the relative political influence of various people in the federal and state government, you're going to have a system that's going to cost more and provide less service."[7]

The master plan laid down comprehensive planning guidelines for California's tripartite system of higher education, consisting of the University of California, the California State University, and the community colleges. The plan defined the roles of the three segments and focused on how to provide educational opportunity to qualified students at a minimal cost.

In 1974, the California Postsecondary Education Commission (CPEC) was created to advise the legislature and the governor on various aspects of postsecondary education. Among their responsibilities is that of reviewing proposals for sites for new UC and CSU institutions. CPEC, said Callan, was created to act as the "steward of the master plan." It was meant, he added, to give "the people who have to respond to the political pressures a

---

[5]From "The California Master Plan of 1960 for Higher Education: an *Ex Ante View*," as quoted in William Chance's *A Vision in Progress: The Decision to Establish a Public University at Monterey Bay*, California Higher Education Policy Center, June 1997.

[6]William Chance, *A Vision in Progress: The Decision to Establish a Public University at Monterey Bay*, California Higher Education Policy Center, June 1997.

[7]Pat Callan, telephone interview, March 1998.

little bit of cover to maneuver." In the California Education Code, the legislature expresses its intent that CPEC have a quasi-regulatory status insofar as its recommendation of new campus sites is needed before authorization of the sites.[8]

Proposals for new institutions are subjected to a three-step review process consisting of (1) the formulation of a long-range plan by each of the three public systems; (2) the submission of a "Letter of Intent to Expand" by the systemwide governing board; and (3) the submission of a "Needs Study" by the systemwide governing board. Proposals are evaluated according to 10 criteria, five of which determine need, four of which determine location, and one that considers economic efficiency. Due to the unusual economic and political pressures surrounding the federal government's offer of the land at Ford Ord, CSU realized it would face great difficulty in fulfilling these criteria.

Stephen R. Reed, CSUMB's associate vice president of university advancement, said that, "The round peg didn't fit in the square hole."[9] Handel Evans described the situation this way:

> The way in which that [the land offer] became an opportunity did not fit the template that everybody in the Legislature or anybody had ever envisaged; that somebody would suddenly . . . come and say, "Look, we've got twelve hundred acres of prime land here in a prime part of the state of California. We're prepared to give it to you. We're also prepared to provide the funding for upgrading it. We know that you have an enormous enrollment problem." You don't build campuses with that sort of beginning; you slowly . . . go through the CPEC guidelines, which take a long, long time. And so what we tried to do was work directly with CPEC in such a way that CPEC had the same sort of involvement, and, I want to say control, but I'll use the word involvement, and do things differently because there was a pressure and an expectation on all of us that we did things differently, that we weren't going to be blocked by some archaic, if I could use that word, but perhaps a better description is "established bureaucracies" that didn't fit a particular picture at that moment in time.

---

[8]Education Code Section 66904.
[9]Stephen R. Reed, telephone interview, March 1998.

Reed echoed this description when he said that the process, "only to some extent followed people's perception of the rules and regulations and policies and procedures that would normally be followed to establish a new campus." The meetings that had commenced and continued between CSU and CPEC throughout the process resulted in what has been described as a new, more cooperative relationship between the two.

IT TAKES TWO TO TANGO

In their report *Breaking Camp—Building a Campus*, CPEC noted that they were willing to tailor their guidelines to the rather unorthodox circumstances in which CSU found itself:

> Because of the magnitude and importance of the Fort Ord Project, the Commission has expressed particular interest in it. Rather than simply responding to the State University's initiatives, it has attempted in part to influence them directly.[10]

> At this stage of deliberations . . . the primary issue is whether or not to accept a sizeable gift of land and buildings from the federal government. Almost all of the other issues surrounding the proposal, those of academic planning, enrollment levels, inter-segmental relations, the provision of student services, and related concerns, are secondary to this consideration, even though they are extremely important in their own right.[11]

Concerning several of these "other issues," namely CPEC's *Guidelines for Review of Proposed University Campuses, Community Colleges, and Educational Centers*, it was evident that CSU would be unable to fulfill them under the pressures of the new time frame. With Monterey residents and the State University wanting their university; the federal government wanting their showcase base conversion; and state legislators knowing they had the opportunity to please everybody, CPEC was under great duress to be accommodating: "In writing guidelines," wrote staff member William

---

[10]CPEC, William L. Storey, contributing staff, Report 94-8, Breaking Camp —Building a Campus, 3, June 1994.

[11]*Ibid.*, 26.

Storey, "the situation invariably arises that does not quite fit the mold, and the proposal to establish California State University, Monterey Bay certainly falls into that category."[12]

Despite the proposal's "uniqueness," continued the report, CPEC's *Guidelines* were, "sufficiently flexible to permit the Commission to follow basic procedures, and consequently to conform quite closely to the spirit of the process, if not exactly to the letter." To the comment that CSU's proposal did not fulfill the guidelines, Evans answered, "Well, it fulfilled them in a different sort of way."

Submission of a systemwide long-range plan, the first step of CPEC's review process, was not forthcoming:

> Unfortunately, the budget crisis of the 1990's have not been conducive to the dispassionate development of long-range designs, and it is therefore not possible to state that the proposal for a new campus in Monterey Bay can be analyzed within the framework of a well-articulated and fully matured state plan.

> However, such a plan is under construction at the present time. . . . The process of developing that report is in its early stages, although some long-range enrollment projections have been developed by the Demographic Research Unit of the Department of Finance, and each of the three public systems is working on its long-range development plans. . . . In one sense, this is a matter of considering the specific prior to the general, which is no one's preference, but in the case at hand, there is little meaningful choice. That review may not be taking place under ideal circumstances, but it must take place nonetheless.[13]

CSU's "Letter of Intent to Expand," submission of which is the second step of the review process, admitted that its own intent, "may not completely fulfill CPEC's guidelines for a Letter of Intent," nevertheless, "CSU believes that it is fulfilling the spirit intended in the guidelines and will fully endeavor to provide additional information as it becomes available." The *Guidelines* require a letter of intent to be submitted, "no less than five years prior to the

---

[12]CPEC, William L. Storey, contributing staff, Report 93-22, *Creating a Campus for the Twenty-first Century*, 44, October 1993.
[13]CPEC.

time it expects the first capital outlay appropriation." The letter was submitted in November 1992; the campus opened in 1995. CPEC justified this dismissal of its procedures by pointing to the fact that the capital outlay appropriation would come not from the state, but from the federal government.

The third step of the review process, development of the needs study, requires the system proposing a new facility to consider alternative sites if land already owned by that system is to be considered for use by the proposed campus. CSU did not own the land at Fort Ord, but they knew that it was theirs for the taking. CSU again used its unique situation to suggest migration from, "the kind of traditional campus planning to which institutions and CPEC are accustomed." Also in the needs study is an admittedly vague vision statement for the new campus:

> In the midst of the budget crisis, while every natural tendency is to protect turf and prerogative, students-faculty-staff are actually imagining a new place to learn, to live, and to work. In that environment it is treacherously simple to call for greater analysis, to point out areas of risk, to ask for earlier approvals, to seek guarantees of success, even to suggest alternative strategies—all necessary and legitimate considerations— while the real challenge is to bring that miracle to life, to provide stronger education, to more people, at lower cost. [14]

CPEC noted that with regard to enrollment projections, "many of the ordinary assumptions about campus expansion do not apply since it is the State University's eventual intention to draw most of its enrollment from outside the area,"[15] another circumstance CPEC described as unique. Concerning enrollment capacities, they claimed, "It is more prudent to compare enrollment projections to existing and scheduled physical capacity than to theoretical planned enrollment capacities that may or may not be reached at some time in the future."[16]

Neither was there a detailed academic plan. Handel Evans said, "We weren't into great depths in the academic program; we were sort of sketching

---

[14]CSU, "CSU Monterey Bay—Planning for a New University at Fort Ord," March 1994, 1-2, as quoted in William Chance's *A Vision in Progress*.

[15]CPEC, Creating a Campus, 39.

[16]CPEC, Breaking Camp.

out a philosophy that talked about cooperation, partnerships." CPEC noted, "An aggressive decision track caused a dilemma that required some flexibility on the part of all concerned, not only in terms of current review, but also with regard to the time schedule for submission of the academic plan." The commission said it would make a detailed review of the already submitted materials and give CSU, "a reasonable amount of time to develop a comprehensive academic plan." Recognizing that no plan existed, CPEC acknowledged that when it did, "a further review—probably through the Commission's program review process—[would] be in order."

William L. Storey, CPEC's chief policy analyst and a contributing staffer to CPEC's reports regarding CSU Monterey Bay, said, "The academic plan in this particular case was flushed out in skeletal form but not really much else."[17] The *Breaking Camp* report stated that,

> The Commission's guidelines require submission of an academic plan. At the present time, no such plan exists. . . . The State University has provided a scenario of how academic program development will probably proceed, and how academic administration will probably be organized. . . . The Commission is optimistic that this vision will be carried out to fruitful levels as the details of the academic plan are developed.[18]

A DIFFERENT SORT OF WAY

What facilitated CPEC's disposition to alter its guidelines was a Memorandum of Understanding (MOU) between CSU and CPEC. The MOU specified the two bodies' intent "to cooperate and collaborate in a joint planning effort, where possible, for general and specific areas of mutual interest" and to generate various "feasibility studies associated with the *Guidelines* document of CPEC."[19]

CPEC's *Creating a Campus for the Twenty-first Century* explained the uncommon step:

---

[17]William L. Storey, telephone interview, April 3, 1998.
[18]CPEC, Breaking Camp.
[19]As quoted in CPEC's Creating a Campus, 35.

Although a Memorandum of Understanding between the Commission and one of the higher education systems is unusual, the policy of cooperation, collaboration, and joint planning is consistent with both the intent and the spirit of the Commission's Guidelines. In all past reviews of proposed new campuses and centers, the Commission has worked cooperatively with the segments in an effort to develop better proposals, and to assure that all proposals serve the needs of California residents. In some cases, it has been determined that a proposal contains conceptual inadequacies sufficient to prevent it from satisfying the Commission's criteria, but in most cases, cooperative planning has produced welcome improvements, and a better planning process.[20]

Consistent with this new spirit of cooperation and collaboration, CSU agreed to provide money for CPEC to assist with joint planning purposes. Defending accusations of "unnatural collusion" between CSU and CPEC, Storey said,

> In the particular case at hand it appeared that there was a new relationship because CPEC and CSU put together an MOU, and had I been asked at the time, because I am the one for CPEC who does this, part of the problem could have been avoided. There was someone . . . who crafted this language that essentially stated that there was a partnership or "joint planning" between CSU and CPEC. That was extremely unfortunate language. Frankly, I exploded when I saw it because it had been done without my advice. . . . It was a very bad mistake. [For some] it confirmed suspicions that there was this sort of unnatural collusion between CSU and CPEC, which was never the case.

Storey went on to say that all this came about at a time when CPEC was in its worst state with regard to its budget. It happened that at the same time governor Pete Wilson was willing to give some planning money to CSU when CPEC's budget was "in the sewer." CPEC Director Warren H. Fox, "saw a way to get $100,000 of that money so that we could sort of carry out what normally would have been our ordinary funded responsibilities," said Storey.

---

[20]CPEC, 36.

143

Vice President Reed, commented that this different way of approving a new campus, "was a hybrid which was either forced or compelled by the unique circumstances." Said Evans,

> We had all the things that we normally have in setting up a university going at the same time. . . All these things were going at once because there was an opportunity that doesn't present itself very often. . . We tried to answer them (the guidelines). In fact we did answer them, but we didn't answer them in the format that were in the initial guidelines. . . We sort of sketched out what we were trying to do in the appropriate committees, and said we understand that this is not in the normal scheme of things the way that you would normally do it, but here's what our idea is.

Reed stressed that "It all went simultaneously rather than in sequence. But, I don't think for one minute that we dodged any of the bullets. I think we did everything we were supposed to, but that we just did it in a different way."

CSU and CPEC officials felt that the land offer of Fort Ord was just too good to pass up. As Storey put it, "How in the world California could have responsibly turned that down I have no idea at all. And we didn't turn it down, and that was the right thing to do." Reed agreed: "It was a take it or leave it proposition and so a decision had to be made quickly or in fact the other community forces would have found another use for the property." The pressure to quickly make this decision coupled with the vague "collective best hunch" of what the prototypical university of the twenty-first century should be suggested to many that CSU

> appeared to have violated that assiduous commitment to planning and in fact knowing all the details before you proceed; in California and in the instance of CSUMB because of the unique circumstances and characteristics of the development. . . . [T]here was an agreement to agree. There was an agreement to proceed before there was an agreement to in fact have an agreed upon curriculum; an agreed upon degree structure; an agreed upon series of unique governance and oversight initiative; marketplace, et cetera, et cetera. There was an agreement to proceed.

Reed did concede that "the violation of known policies and procedures in fact meant that some important aspect of consideration was minimized."

In response to comments that this was an agreement to proceed in light of the fact that no guidelines had been fulfilled, Reed replied: "I wouldn't say *no* [guidelines were fulfilled]. There were more *X*'s in the equation than givens." Nor, he said, was it a case of just pushing through the proposal in order to get the land from the federal government:

> This stuff came at CPEC very, very quickly. That's not to say that it came as a consequence of poor decision-making or neglectful timing. We were asked, we think, by the state of California, *in toto*, to behave swiftly, flexibly, to work hard and to move fast, and in fact, to do what many people thought was impossible, which was to open a campus in a very, very short period of time and to do so with . . . appropriate innovation and uniqueness. We did. And we are. And it's a work in progress.

Critics of the process and outcome contend the teaching at CSUMB is too soft and unstructured, that too many radical and unconventional teachers find the curriculum attractive, and that this is precisely the opposite of what is needed to provide undereducated young people with needed job skills.

Vice President Hendrickson agreed with his colleague's enthusiasm:

> It was a commitment we made and it was a commitment at this point, as I look back on it, that was well founded, and it paid off. And we've done something I think that's unique, not only in building an educational institution, but . . . doing it with all the damn bureaucracy we had to go through. . . . It's absolutely unbelievable. Had we not had people believing in what in the hell we were doing, and I mean they believed in it, we would never have succeeded. No way in hell. We had the right people forcing it through the system.

IV. Implementation and Oversight

Case 10

INTRODUCTION

Proponents of redevelopment argue it is a win-win that should be used liberally and widely. Critics claim it is an investment tool that benefits business people at the expense of state taxpayers and local residents dependent on public services. Perhaps, given the situation, it could be either, neither, or both.

This is a powerful case—*a tale of two cities*—that demonstrates with clarity the degree to which good policy intentions can go awry in the implementation. Who was responsible in this case? Was there adequate oversight? Should state legislators who passed the legislation have anticipated the problems? It has been said that all politics is local, but are state representatives likely to stand up to manipulative local agencies within their districts?

On its face, *The Blighted Desert* seems far more a description of the frailties of human nature than a story of *malice,* in the case of Indian Wells, or of *foolish pride,* in the case of Coachella. Residents of one community persuaded themselves that their creativity and prosperity helped neighbors outside their immediate area; why weren't their neighbors grateful? Leaders in the other community persuaded themselves that there were underlying values that forced them to "let the perfect drive out the good." Rejecting the offer as an act of malice on the part of the wealthier community, how would you describe the effect the offer of funds had on the Latino community? Are you prepared to dismiss the possibility of a deliberate "divide and conquer" strategy? What of the media's condemnation of the rejection? What of the references to the gender of some of the Coachella council members?

Are the Indian Wells officials correct in pointing out the economic advantages of using limited funds for low-income housing in low-income areas? Are the Coachella officials correct in contending that Indian Wells residents are saying, in effect, "We will pay you to keep away?" How can they both be right? What did the legislation intend? Was it ambiguous enough to claim both conflicting goals? How does legislation so ambiguous pass? Or, does ambiguity lubricate passage by allowing people on opposite sides to claim a win in its passage? If many different interpretations are possible in the implementation phase, to whom does this transfer power? Local agencies? The courts?

Note well the presence of fundamental conflicting values: Larger numbers of low-income units in less wealthy areas promote economic egalitarianism; but cut heavily against social egalitarianism. You would do well to secure a good grasp of the arguments made by the leaders in the two communities.

What does the Marriott-Bone controversy teach you about the orderliness of public decision making? Do personal attributes count? Do relationships matter? Should you always, sometimes, or rarely take such things into consideration? Can you afford not to?

Critics of *The Blighted Desert* case contend that most redevelopment agencies generally carry out their tasks well—including the provision of low-income housing within their boundaries—and that the case is an isolated one that is factually unique. Legislative efforts at reform—some successful, some not—militate against the first point. It is hard to imagine wealthy communities that want to eliminate blight embracing their low-income neighbors with much enthusiasm. As to the second point, there are other "blighted communities" of high wealth in California, like Coronado and Palos Verde. But even if it were factually unique, the case could be a good learning tool. Didn't the unprecedented tragic explosion of the Challenger Space Shuttle teach us a lesson or two?

Creative Evasion: The Blighted Desert

Research and original writing by Senate Associate Joshua Hamilton

THE VALLEY

Not far from the teeming urban canyons of Los Angeles lies a vast desert. The Coachella Valley nestles in a wash of the San Jacinto and San Bernardino Mountains. When the spring rains hit the mountains, muddy brown water races down in rivulets, flooding gullies and sweeping into the dry riverbeds. Most of the year, the valley's hard clay soil supports little vegetation except scrub brush and occasional colonies of Joshua trees.

The Hollywood elite of the early 1920s considered the Coachella Valley a sanctuary, a quiet haven, even then, from the rush of city life. Charlie Farrell's Racquet Club in Palm Springs lured a gaudy list of silver screen luminaries. Greta Garbo, Clark Gable, and Errol Flynn shared the sun-drenched poolside. Later, Frank Sinatra and his Rat Pack performed in Palm Springs nightspots and built stylish homes in the pristine desert outside town. Today, the Coachella Valley remains a haven for the wealthy.

It also attracts smog-choked Angelenos seeking a quiet vacation, especially those desirous of soothing their aging and aching joints in the warm air. Responsive developers have turned the hard red ground of the desert into a verdant garden of golf courses for wealthy visitors and permanent retirees. Tens of thousands of carefully trimmed green acres cover the valley today. At least 50,000 swimming pools cool vacationers under the hot desert sun. While tourism is the region's economic powerhouse, the continuing influx of retirees has more than doubled the valley's population in the last 15 years.

Although seasonal statistics vary, the number of year-round residents in the valley is modest. Some 260,000 residents live in nine municipalities in the 30-mile long valley, all in Riverside County. The cities are strung like pearls on a chain down the center of the valley, not far from Interstate 10 as it runs southeast into the Mojave Desert.

The Coachella Valley is a region of contrasts. "We have some of the wealthiest cities in America and some of the poorest. We have families who live in shacks, fields, and under trees, and we have people who live in 40,000 square foot homes" said John Mealey, executive director of the Coachella Valley Housing Coalition.[1]

The south end of the valley is mostly Latino, the north is Anglo. Like an antebellum plantation economy, the valley relies on a large base of menial, low-paying jobs to maintain the level of comfort that vacationers and retirees expect. Nestled in the southern portion of the desert lie the two cities of Indian Wells and Coachella. Perhaps two cities, so close, have never been so different.

A TALE OF TWO CITIES

Indian Wells is one of the wealthiest cities in California. Coachella is one of the poorest. The average resident of Indian Wells is 62 years of age. The average Coachellan is 23. Indian Wells had 2,600 residents in 1990—95 percent white, with no African Americans. Coachella, with 20,000 residents, also had few African Americans, and few whites as well—it is virtually all Latino. Despite their differences in population, municipal revenues in Indian Wells were almost four times greater than in Coachella in 1990.

The median household income in this enclave is estimated at $100,000. More than 75 percent of the residents live behind guarded gates including Bob Hope, Jimmy Stewart, Lee Iaccoca, Bill Gates, and John Elway. The city, with no overhead power lines, noisy school yards, or gas stations, is a far cry from its sun burnt Coachella neighbor 10 miles to the east.

FISCAL APOCALYPSE

The city of Indian Wells' financial situation has not always been as healthy as that of its residents. In 1978, with the passage of Proposition 13, the fiscal landscape for local government completely changed. The new law limited the ability of local governments to collect property taxes, and

---

[1] Interview, April 17, 2000.

many cities and counties saw revenue drop 60 percent. It hit Indian Wells, one of the wealthiest per capita cities, especially hard. With little commercial or retail development, Indian Wells financed itself with building fees and property taxes paid by high-end resorts and retirees.

Over time, most cities tried to make up for lost revenue by using marketing, zoning, and other lures to entice businesses whose activities produce high sales tax revenues. Not so Indian Wells. It did not want to compromise its "residential feel." Indian Wells kept retail business out and began charging residents fees for municipal services. There was little, if any, objection on the part of residents. In fact, the fees generated so much excess money that it was placed in an account whose interest was expected to finance city services in perpetuity. Then, in 1980, came Proposition 4, the Gann Initiative. Designed to protect city dwellers unwilling to pay the fees, as opposed to those of Indian Wells, it prohibited cities from charging fees greater than the cost of services, and it required them to spend accumulated funds within 10 years. Indian Wells city officials estimated that, pursuant to those rules, the city would be bankrupt by 1985. It soon ran up the largest per-capita debt in the Coachella Valley—more than $10,000 for every man, woman and child. As City Manager George Watts put it, "We were on the brink of insolvency."[2] In 1983, the desperate city dusted off a 1945 law, formed a redevelopment agency, and declared one of the wealthiest and most beautiful spots on the earth a blighted community.

BENEVOLENT SLUM LORDS

Post-World War II Californians, faced with aging downtown cores, ugly slums, boarded-up businesses, and a housing shortage, approved a sweeping redevelopment law. A 1944 Los Angeles Town Hall Report noted:

> The decay of large areas in American cities, notably in the central sections, is one of the major problems of today. Blight and slums have spread over an estimated one-fourth of the urban America. . . . In Los Angeles, for example there has been a decrease of approximately three-

---

[2]Interview, April 12, 2000.

quarters of a billion dollars in the assessed valuation of property during the past decade.[3]

The new law created a hybrid institution—a state-authorized program implemented by local governments. Local entities known as redevelopment agencies would follow legislative guidelines reflecting the intent of the redevelopment law. Beyond that, the local governments that created the agencies would guide them. For example, and quite typically, a city council would form a redevelopment agency and appoint its members to the governing board. The council would make policy decisions on urban problems, and the agency board would implement them. But in Indian Wells, the city council was the redevelopment agency. Glen Campora, of the state Department of Housing and Community Development, said: "Sacramento has chosen to leave redevelopment agencies in the same vein as city councils." State policymakers were reluctant to micromanage local government.

Since 1951, redevelopment agencies have financed themselves through "tax increment financing." This theory assumes that a "revitalized project area will generate more property taxes than were being produced before redevelopment."[4] The tax valuation of a project area prior to redevelopment activity is the "base" number. As the redevelopment project improves the property, the increase in taxes beyond the "base" is the redevelopment agency's profit. As the redevelopment agency captures additional tax money generated within its borders, it takes not only money that would have gone to the city, but money that normally would go to other taxing agencies like school districts, special districts, counties, and the state. The state "backfills" the lost revenue to schools, but not to other entities. They are net losers to redevelopment.

In 1998 redevelopment agencies captured about $1.6 billion in taxes that would have gone to other public agencies. Because schools use about half of this money, $800 million temporarily lost to schools through this capture, was backfilled. The net effect was that the state granted redevelopment agencies $800 million in subsidies and other local governments granted them another $800 million in subsidies.

---

[3]David Beatty, *Redevelopment in California,* 2nd edition, 1995, 2.
[4]*Id.*, at 186.

Any city or county can establish a redevelopment agency by simply declaring a need for one. The redevelopment agency then draws boundaries around pockets of blight and designates specific redevelopment "project areas." The aim is to attract businesses to the areas designated for improvement. Local redevelopment agencies have extraordinary powers granted by the state. They can acquire land through eminent domain, develop or sell property, and secure financing through bond sales to the state or federal government. In a 1993 amendment, "blight" was generously defined. It could include not only rundown properties needing attention, but any physical or economic condition that would hinder private enterprise. Blight, in other words, was in the eye of the beholder.

So, while Proposition 13 forced local governments and schools to get a two-thirds vote to increase taxes or issue bonds, it did not apply to tax increment financed redevelopment agencies. A city council, "with the bang of a gavel," can reconvene as a redevelopment agency, sell bonds, and capture tax dollars for civic projects with a simple majority vote.

THE ESTRANGED COUPLE

One major constraint on redevelopment agencies is the need to construct low-income housing. Addressing fears that, by eradicating slums, redevelopment activity was decreasing the housing stock for the poor, the legislature passed a law in 1977 requiring that 20 percent of all tax dollars generated by the redevelopment agency be used to construct low and moderate income housing within the project area. About the same time, the legislature mandated that every unit bulldozed be replaced. The mandate created one of the strongest and most reliable sources of low-income housing in the state. In 1992-93, redevelopment agencies spent approximately $370 million on low-income housing, building a total of 7,801 units. "Redevelopment agencies are the single most important source for affordable housing in the state," said Glen Campora at the Department of Housing and Community Development.[5]

Despite the success in building homes, the estrangement between redevelopment agencies and the housing requirement is palpable. The agencies are created to raze buildings and alter the physical landscape with the sole intent of creating wealth. Redevelopment officials don't like

---

[5]Interview, April 14, 2000.

being forced to spend a significant portion of their revenues on low-income housing. They view it as an economic loser when the city could be zoning in Wal-Marts or auto malls.

According to Marc Brown with the California Rural Legal Assistance Foundation, some redevelopment agencies will sit on their housing funds and then seek to spend them on anything but housing. "We have redevelopment agencies spending their housing dollars on street lights—and they don't even try to justify it."[6]

Housing standards for redevelopment agencies complement state law requiring cities to zone housing for all income types. The state has designated four categories: very low income, low income, moderate income, and everyone else. These designations are meant to increase socio-economic and racial integration and distribute the low-income housing burden evenly among local governments. Brown said: "There is a principle of getting more affordable housing built, but there is also a strategy in making sure there is a racial and economic mix in a neighborhood."

KING PLAYING PEASANT

To combat its impending "insolvency," Indian Wells formed a redevelopment agency in 1983. At the time, the code description of blight was expansive. It included any condition that posed a roadblock to capital investment by the business community, not necessarily disrepair. For example, the lack of adequate infrastructure could be considered a barrier.

The city council of Indian Wells, acting as its Redevelopment Agency Board, in what some regard as the most creative construction of legislative intent on record, declared an open, pristine desert "blighted" because it lacked adequate flood control. According to Indian Wells, this lack of infrastructure was a hindrance to future capital investment and legitimized redeveloping an undeveloped parcel of land. Indian Wells city manager George Watts said, "When the redevelopment agency was formed, . . . it was done by the letter of the law during the time. It was perfectly legal."[7]

In addition to providing flood control, the redevelopment agency began a more controversial project—a 36-hole luxury golf course within the

---

[6]Interview, April 10, 2000.
[7]Interview, April 12, 2000.

blighted area. It concluded that the city would be unable to attract a high-end resort to its blighted area without offering developers the incentive of 36 holes of championship quality golf. Thus, Indian Wells came to have hundreds of acres of desert and golf course blight.

This Keynesian approach to golf worked. Indian Wells ultimately succeeded in luring two luxury hotels, a Hyatt and a Stouffers with a combined value of $800 million dollars, to fix a blighted golf course that had fixed a blighted desert. In 1987, voters in Indian Wells approved a one billion dollar resort complex to fix the now-blighted hotel area. To be built by Sunterra Development Company, the resort would include a 2,500 to 3,000-room luxury hotel; three more golf courses; a tennis center; a 30-acre village of shops and restaurants; and a 400,000 square foot convention center—all located within the redevelopment agency zone. Each project would bring an estimated 10,000 low-paying jobs, and ultimately tens of millions of dollars into Indian Wells.

SOWING THE GRAPES OF WRATH

By 1988, leisure activities at Indian Wells were first-rate. One redevelopment agency golf course hosted a nationally televised tournament. A brand new $45-million twin tower high-rise condo complex, complete with concierge service, was selling its $1,895,000 priced units at a brisk pace.

Meanwhile, Coachella, the forgotten urchin of the valley, was attracting little investment. Its hopes were dashed when Jessica Hahn was discovered to have been the mistress of nationally prominent televangelist Jim Bakker. Bakker, charged with tax evasion, and abandoned by his wife and business partner, Tammy Faye, canceled plans to build a religious theme park in Coachella.

Officially contemplated in the billion dollar Sunterra project were 750 housing units to fulfill the city's low-income housing requirements. It was hardly enough to accommodate the thousands of workers employed by the resorts, but the developer did it as a good will gesture. When Indian Wells residents heard about the proposal, modest as it was, they protested and the city council balked. To soothe its residents' fears, Indian Wells proposed that the units be built outside the city in an unincorporated part of Riverside County. The actual distance was not great; the units would go in on the other side of the freeway from Indian Wells. And, after all, it was new housing designated for low-income families. Still, something bothered the designated beneficiaries. It was the motivation that angered housing advocates in the Coachella Valley.

Units financed with redevelopment dollars, would be used to satisfy Indian Wells' low-income housing requirements. CRLA attorney Marc Brown and the Western Center for Law and Poverty charged that siting them outside of Indian Wells had racist and classist undertones. Brown sued to have the 750 units built within the physical boundaries of Indian Wells.

Indian Wells stonewalled. The city called in its lawyers and declared its readiness to fight. Clearly outgunned and faced with an appeals process that could last for years, housing advocates entered into a pact with Indian Wells. Compromise, they reasoned, would do more to help the poor in the valley than a prolonged legal battle. And housing would be far cheaper to build outside of Indian Wells. It would house more people and address the regional housing shortage.[8] As part of the compromise, Indian Wells agreed to allow 100 low-income units in Indian Wells and sweetened the deal by doubling the number of units built outside to 1,350. It was an agreeable compromise, except for one small problem. It was against the law. The 1977 law would have to be amended to allow redevelopment agencies to transfer low-income housing dollars outside the redevelopment boundaries.

BOB PRESLEY

The man for the job was the local state senator, Bob Presley. Former undersheriff of Riverside County, Presley was known for his pragmatism and ability to get things done. Both sides asked him to carry the bill, assured him the changes were minor and noncontroversial, and that the differences between them had been worked out. CRLA and the Western Center for Law and Poverty agreed to officially support the bill. Presley saw it as "a bill you would do in your spare time, something you would send a staff member to present in committee."[9] No one foresaw that the bill would erupt into an ego clash between two major resorts in Indian Wells and catapult the reclusive community into statewide news.

---

[8]Marc Brown, interview, April 14, 2000.
[9]Senator Bob Presley, interview, April 17, 2000.

The bill was deceptively simple and site-specific. Indian Wells Redevelopment Agency would be allowed to spend its low- and moderate-income housing funds outside the city if the agency met 11 requirements. It would be the first exception to the 10-year old law, but the bill was crafted only to apply to Indian Wells. The application was limited, but were its ramifications? Housing advocates saw the bill as a compromise that created an opportunity to build hundreds of affordable housing units where few existed.

Seeing the odd bedfellows surprised a hitherto dormant power. Marriott realized that if the legislation passed, the new Sunterra project would be built right beside its hotel. Fearing competition, they were determined to kill the compromise. Then, they reasoned, Indian Wells would cancel the project rather than be forced to accommodate low-income housing within its borders.

Sunterra developer Bill Bone, who had developed the Marriott complex, had assured Marriott that he would not build another resort nearby. When Bone proposed his billion dollar project, Marriott zeroed in on the Presley bill.

"It became a bitter personal fight between Bone and Marriott," said Senator Presley, "What surprised me was how both sides hired all these lobbyists to kill something that I considered just to be a minor bill."[10] Said Brown, "These two guys had an ego clash and by the time it got over to the Assembly, it was just strange."

In those early days of April, the capitol was in a frenzy over this minor issue. Marriott and Sunterra assembled legions of high-priced lobbyists and lathered politicians with campaign contributions. Presley remembered: "Marriott told their guys to hire all the lobbyists they needed and that money was not an object." Marriott weighed in with $32,500 in campaign contributions—and 13 of the 16 members who received contributions either opposed the bill or abstained. Not to be outdone, Bone lavished over $400,000 dollars on senators and assembly members, and spent $21,700 on trips so senators could "investigate the blight in Indian Wells" first hand.

Meanwhile, the Capitol press corps began to see similarities with apartheid in South Africa. One senator began asking his colleagues if they had voted on Presley's "Soweto Bill."

---

[10]Interview, April 17, 2000.

Indian Wells Mayor Richard Oliphant was incredulous: "It [was] like getting up on stage and announcing that you want to do some good and everyone throws rocks and tomatoes at you." Despite the high profile controversy, the bill passed the senate and assembly rather easily and landed on Governor Deukmejian's desk. To everyone's surprise, including Presley's, he vetoed it.

In his veto message, the governor said the bill would have "statewide ramifications far beyond the boundaries of Indian Wells and the County of Riverside." It would set a "precedent to permit redevelopment funds to … be spent beyond the project jurisdiction."[11] The anticlimactic ending sent each side packing and left Indian Wells with the prospect of having to find room for affordable housing in its city. Unlike the bill, however, the controversy did not die. It touched off a healthy debate over housing and redevelopment agencies.

THE '90s, YEA!

As late as 1993, the dust had not yet settled in Indian Wells. The low-income housing project was still in the planning stages. The 750-unit complex had been downsized into a 90-unit senior housing project, but the details were still being worked out and completion was not expected for another year. To complicate matters, the high intensity lobbying campaign by Marriott and Sunterra became involved in a bribery scandal with legislators sent to prison effectively for selling their votes.

Around this time, California was in the midst of a severe economic recession. A drought and a freeze gripped its agribusiness industries. Aerospace corporations were pulling out of southern California. The housing crisis in the Coachella Valley was so bad that hotels in Indian Wells were sending buses 40 miles to Banning and Beaumont to pick up workers.[12]

The impoverished state government was raiding the bank accounts of local governments and redevelopment agencies to meet budgetary minimums and provide basic services. As a supposed good will gesture, redevelopment agencies from wealthy jurisdictions sent representatives to walk the halls of the capitol offering to give the state money from their low-

---

[11]Veto Message, May 24, 1988.
[12]Interview, John Mealey, April 17, 2000.

income housing funds. "They were not giving up their 80 percent of the money, just their 20 percent housing set-aside," said Marc Brown. [13] By 1993, California faced a housing shortage, and many local governments envied the low-income housing dollars idling in neighboring redevelopment agencies. By law, of course, the agencies could only spend the funds within their boundaries. After proposals by Indian Wells and other cities to transfer funds out of their jurisdictions, the legislature began to wonder if its housing mandate was rigid and arbitrary given statewide housing needs. Legislators began to suggest that a mechanism should be introduced to allow transfers of housing funds outside redevelopment areas. Bill Arenstein, mayor of Indian Wells and president of the Coachella Valley Association of Governments, began to lobby legislators to allow smaller geographic regions like the Coachella Valley to "develop voluntary model programs and . . . share expenses and coordinate housing assistance" irrespective of municipal boundaries.[14] His suggestions were incorporated into a Senate Local Government Interim Hearing, and, in 1993, the time was right for this debate. Senator Marian Bergeson, chair of the Senate Local Government Committee, introduced a bill to allow transfers between jurisdictions.

Low-income housing advocates were concerned that the bill would exacerbate the separation of economic and racial groups by allowing wealthy communities to export their low-income housing requirements to other cities. But they were ambivalent. Housing was an integral component of redevelopment law, and housing advocates did not want it to lose its saliency. Flexibility seemed necessary. Despite the concerns of housing advocates, lawmakers moved the Bergeson bill through both houses of the legislature.

While the bill was in conference committee, Marc Brown met with Bergeson and other lawmakers to hammer out the stipulations that would allow transfers. What emerged from those meetings was a set of 23 conditions set by fair housing advocates that did not compromise the state's housing ideals while allowing transfers in narrow circumstances. The terms were so stringent that Peter Detwiler joked that it was a "good news/bad

---

[13]Interview, April 14, 2000.

[14]Redevelopment Agencies' Housing Programs: A Summary Report from the Interim Hearings of the Senate Committee on Local Government, December 17, 1991, 83.

news" scenario in which we "finally had a law that would allow transfers, but it was so complicated that nobody would ever be able to use it." To his credit, no one ever has.

EATING CAKE

By 1996, Indian Wells had completed its gated, 90-unit, low-income senior housing project. Although most redevelopment agencies spend 10-20 percent of their low-income housing funds on a project and supplement the remainder with other funds, Indian Wells spent all of their housing funds on this one project[15]—$13.6 million dollars on a 90-unit complex, making it one of the most expensive in the state.

But the redevelopment agency was generating handsome returns for the city. The original project area, assessed at $397 million dollars in 1983, was now worth approximately $1.3 billion and generated an estimated $15 million in revenue. Unfortunately, Indian Wells was also on the top 10 list of those redevelopment agencies with the highest amount of funds in their low-income housing accounts.[16]

Indian Wells Redevelopment Agency announced in 1996 that it would pay $10 million dollars from its agency funds to subsidize flood control facilities for a developer building a prestigious resort. According to its marketing brochure, ownership at this resort, called "The Reserve," would only be open to a "select and prominent group." It would consume 500 acres of open desert, include a luxury golf course, and provide future residents with a fiber optic line for fast Internet connections. Perhaps this feature was what enticed Bill Gates to purchase an undeveloped home lot in "The Reserve" for $1.35 million.

This influx of cash meant that Indian Wells was accumulating even more money in its low-income housing fund. In 1997, Senator David Kelley, who represented the Coachella area, introduced a bill that would allow 10 specified jurisdictions in the valley, including Indian Wells and Coachella, to transfer low- income housing funds among themselves to address housing needs on a regional level. It was marketed as a pragmatic approach that would increase the total supply of housing in the valley by

---

[15]Interview, John Mealey, April 17, 2000.

[16]*End or Means? Redevelopment Agencies' Housing Program*, Interim Hearings of the Senate Committee on Local Government, November 13, 1996, 12.

maximizing the number of units built. After all, the asking price for a cheap undeveloped acre was $150,000 in Indian Wells; but only $10,000 in Coachella. And pooling low-income housing money regionally would increase financial capability.

Some wealthy communities that had been sitting on low-income housing funds for years took advantage of the bill. Officials from the Coachella Valley Association of Governments, which sponsored the bill, approached Coachella City Councilwoman Silvia Montenegro and asked her to support the bill. They told her "Coachella would be the perfect place for Indian Wells to transfer its low-income housing funds because the community was so poor," Montenegro said. But Kelley eventually dropped the bill: the same tensions that had surfaced in 1988 about exclusive communities building low-income housing remained 10 years later.

Indian Wells was also becoming embroiled in another controversy with its low-income housing funds. After settling out of court for shorting Riverside County $7.4 million in redevelopment payments, Indian Wells was now trying to redefine how its 20 percent set aside for low-income housing would be determined.[17] As stated by law and reinforced by an Attorney general's opinion, the low-income housing amount is based on the gross amount of redevelopment agency revenue. After the low-income housing amount is determined, the redevelopment agency may begin to pay its other financial obligations. Indian Wells wanted to change the law and determine its 20 percent set aside after other obligations had been met. That slight change would have decreased its obligation to low-income housing by a million dollars a year.[18] Low-income housing advocates intervened and Indian Wells retreated, but not before the scheme made the local newspapers.

. . . AND HAVING IT TOO

In Indian Wells, the fly in the redevelopment ointment has always been housing; the more money they make, the more they have to set aside for something they see as a fiscal loser. In early 1999, Indian Wells began a

---

[17]"Indian Wells to Pay 7 Million," *Riverside Press Enterprise*, March 14, 1998.

[18]"Low-Income Housing was the Goal, Large Scale Avoidance is the Result," *Riverside Press Enterprise*, March 27, 1997.

dialogue with city councilmembers from Coachella about accepting a direct transfer of its excess low-income housing funds using the 1993 Bergeson bill with its 23 stipulations. This would be the first to attempt to crack Bergeson's legislative code.

Indian Wells approached Coachella Councilmembers Gilbert Ramirez, Juan DeLara, and Richard Macknicki. Indian Wells had over $13 million in its low-income housing account and wanted to transfer the maximum amount allowed by the Bergeson bill: $1.5 million. Absent from the initial communications were Silvia Montenegro and Lupia Dominguez, the other two Coachella councilmembers. Eventually, the proposal was publicly announced and people in Coachella were excited about the possibility of $1.5 million being invested in their poor community. "I believe it is our responsibility to our people to take advantage of this" Councilman Ramirez remarked. "Think of those who have an $8,000 house because they bought it in the 1920s and grandmother is still living there, but there is never enough money to fix the roof."[19]

As in 1988 and 1997, and now in 1999, Indian Wells argued that high property values and a lack of available land made its city a poor site for low-income housing. Low-income housing lawyers countered, as they had in earlier years, that Indian Wells was again trying to export its responsibility to house its service workers. Many in Coachella were against it, including Coachella resident Pat Otten: "We are proud workers; we are not so low-living that we don't know what is right and what is wrong," she said.[20] Despite perfunctory opposition, however, low-income housing advocates were relatively mute compared to their past protests.

As soon as the proposal was made, the City Council of Indian Wells voted unanimously to transfer the money to Coachella. As prescribed by the Bergeson bill, the onus was now on the Coachella City Council to accept the funds. With elections a few months away, the acceptance became a central issue in the campaign.

Previously supportive councilmembers campaigned heavily in favor of accepting the "gift" from Indian Wells. They had a good point. One-and-a-half million dollars would do little in Indian Wells, but would go a long way in Coachella to rebuild 150 aging homes for some of the valleys' poorest residents. If the money stayed in Indian Wells, it would be spent

---

[19]"Rich Cities Funds are Hot Potato," *Los Angeles Times*, October 27, 1999.
[20]*Ibid.*

on another senior project and would not benefit service workers or serve to racially integrate Indian Wells. Said Jonathan Lehrer-Graiwer, a housing lawyer who supported the transfer, "Indian Wells will fry before they build low-income housing for families, and Coachella can use the money."

"We feel strongly that because we are affluent and the coffers are full, we have a moral responsibility to help others," responded Indian Wells Mayor Artie Henderson.[21] Added City Manager George Watts, "If Coachella doesn't want the money, we'll keep it here and build senior units. But the state is trying to force low-income housing where many low-income people don't want to live. We were not trying to get around any requirements. We have plans to purchase property and build another senior complex. The question is, where would this money go further?"[22]

SYLVIA MONTENEGRO

Sylvia Montenegro was a Coachella city councilwoman elected by one vote in 1973. She was a founder of the Coachella Valley Housing Coalition and remains an advocate for fair housing practices by local governments. Where other poor communities in the valley, like Indio, have put moratoriums on new low-income family housing, Montenegro has been instrumental in putting more low-income housing units in Coachella than any other city in the valley.

Montenegro came out strongly against the Indian Wells proposal. "This is a racist, classist decision on behalf of Indian Wells," she said. Montenegro and her protégé, Councilmember candidate Rosanna Contreras, campaigned against the proposed transfer. "I believe that Indian Wells must accept its responsibility according to statute," Montenegro said. "When Indian Wells formed the redevelopment agency, they knew exactly what they were doing. . . . That was their choice. The statutes that govern Indian Wells are the same that govern Coachella. What they have done is build some housing for seniors, but certainly the seniors in my community could not live there."[23] Montenegro defined the context of the debate.

The candidates brought their messages to the town halls and civic clubs of Coachella, and on November 2, 1999, voters in Coachella elected a new

---

[21]"Rich Cities Funds are Hot Potato," *Los Angeles Times*, October 27, 1999.
[22]Interview, April 12, 2000.
[23]Interview, April 11, 2000.

city council. Of approximately 30,000 residents, 846 Coachellans went to the polls to cast their ballot. As the returns came in, it was evident that the race would be close. When the vote was finally tallied, Rosanna Contreras had defeated Richard MacKnicki by a single vote. The balance in the council had shifted against the transfer and the new council appointed Councilwoman Montenegro mayor. The new female-majority council was sworn in and voted on December 1 to reject the transfer. "Gilbert Ramirez and DeLara were vehement about receiving the money because they had made it a central campaign pledge. It was their project," said Montenegro. The candidates had run on how they would vote and further debate was futile. The council defeated the proposal 3-2 with Montenegro, Contreras, and Dominguez voting against it and DeLara and Ramirez voting in favor. The rejection sowed confusion in Coachella. Many people were angry that a town as poor as Coachella would have the audacity to turn away $1.5 million. "There were many people who have called them [Indian Wells] racist and have thanked us for not accepting the dregs off their table," Montenegro said. "They felt it was a show of leadership not to accept the money. Others say, 'We are so poor, why did you not accept the money?'."[24] The Palm Springs *Desert Sun* ran an editorial condemning the actions of Coachella's new city council and criticisms rained down for throwing away money on principle. Rosanna Contreras was especially castigated, and Councilman DeLara called another vote on the matter.

The Bergeson bill had a sunset date of December 31, 1999. After that, it would expire and the only mechanism redevelopment agencies had to send their money elsewhere would end. Indian Wells had to meet the New Year's deadline if the transfer were to take place.

At a December 29 meeting of the Coachella City Council, the last before the New Year, Juan DeLara asked for a revote on the transfer. Bowing to intense criticism and scrutiny, the newest member on the council, Rosanna Contreras changed her vote and approved the transfer from Indian Wells.

ENTER HCD

As required by Bergeson, the Department of Housing and Community Development (HCD) must review any proposed transfer to determine whether or not the 23 prerequisites were met. HCD is the only agency with

---

[24]Silvia Montenegro, interview, April 11, 2000.

oversight over these transactions, but its power is limited. HCD can only "report findings" and "identify noncompliant issues."[25] Even if HCD found Indian Wells in violation of the law, Coachella still could have accepted and used the funds. HCD had been tracking the situation at the request of Indian Wells but had not made a public statement on the issue prior to the Coachella City Council vote.

Indian Wells had submitted a report to the Department of Housing and Community Development on October 21 detailing its compliance with all 23 conditions of the law. The toughest of the 23 conditions was that the donating community had to be in compliance with its low-income housing requirements. Indian Wells asserted that its obligation had been met by the 90-unit senior housing complex and house cleaners' cottages behind many of the homes. Officials cited $13 million dollars earmarked for another senior housing project to be completed in 2001.

The department report was damning. Glen Campora, who reviewed the transfer, said: "The legislature put in declaratory language to show the intent and spirit of the law. Housing law requires that cities zone for all income groups. Although Indian Wells had enough low-income through their senior housing, they were not in compliance with the spirit of the law to provide housing for all income types, including their service workers." HCD found that Indian Wells not only had not met the letter of the law,[26] but was out of compliance with the spirit of the law. "The legislature intended affordable housing for all, not just particular segments of society, such as seniors," said Campora. Notwithstanding this disregard of the law, HCD had no authority to act.

But HCD's report became the "shot heard round the valley." Officials at Indian Wells were angered that a state bureaucracy would interpret legislative intent: "They [the HCD] were against it in the first place. We met the requirements, but HCD nitpicked at it. They had a bias about allowing the transfer. It was our understanding that the law was put there so the people who were against the law could make it so stringent that no city could qualify to do it. There was a laundry list of requirements that most cities could not meet."[27] Marc Brown, who had helped Senator

---

[25]Glen Campora, interview, April 14, 2000.

[26]It specifically had not met conditions 1-3, 13 or 19, according to Glen Campora of HCD.

[27]Interview, April 12, 2000.

Bergeson craft the bill admitted: "Individually all of the 23 conditions make sense, but together . . . it would be kind of hard for a city to [comply with]."[28]

DENOUEMENT

Sylvia Montenegro had not changed her stance, and the HCD report steeled her against the transfer. Mayor Montenegro said: "As soon as we received the printouts from HCD, all the members of the council now had all the facts. As soon as Councilwoman Contreras read the HCD report, she called for another city council meeting." At that meeting in early January 2000, Councilwoman Contreras called another vote on the transfer. Armed with the HCD's report, she changed her vote and the proposal was defeated.

Again, local press and community leaders condemned the vote. The Coachella Planning Commission had already made plans for the money and was angered that the council let $1.5 million slip through its fingers. "The press had a wonderful time with this," said Montenegro. "They made it appear that the ladies of Coachella had not the inkling of what the entire matter was about. They said, what were these women thinking—that's what happens when women are in office. What really happened was that once the council was properly informed of the situation, the majority of the council made the right choice. It wasn't emotional; it was because a majority of the council chose to uphold the statute."[29] The final rejection by Coachella occurred after the Bergeson bill sunset and marked the end of all attempts to receive low- income housing funds from Indian Wells.

Again, officials in Indian Wells were incredulous. "Their rejection had nothing to do with benefitting or not benefitting Coachella residents, and everything to do with politics," said City Manager George Watts.

Sylvia Montenegro's position was: "We are going to hold your feet to the fire, Indian Wells. We are going to make you build all your required units in Indian Wells." Well, whom do you hurt here? The entire affordable housing law was to help the neediest people in the neediest areas. It's not for Indian Wells. This woman and her companions decided that they are

---

[28]*Ibid.*

[29]Interview, April 11, 2000.

going to stand on principle and require Indian Wells to build all its required units. That's fine. We are going to do it, and we are prepared to do it.[30]

The Coachella City Council had other reasons for rejecting the money. The HCD report was sufficiently damning that even if Coachella accepted the money, the attorney general would likely challenge the transfer and the issue could remain in court for years. Coachella would not be guaranteed the money, but the $1.5 million would be credited to its account when applying to the federal government or other sources of housing funds. With the threat of a prolonged legal challenge and a decreased leverage to procure additional funds, the $1.5 million seemed to be more of a burden than a blessing. Montenegro said, "I don't see how we can hold up all we are doing for housing to wait for $1.5 million."[31]

The majority of the Coachella Council agreed with HCD's conclusion that Indian Wells had not complied with its housing mandate. However, rejection of the funds had as much to do with the practicality of accepting the funds as it did with the principle of rejecting them. "In order for a city to transfer its L&M funds, the donor city must have complied with its share of affordable housing, and to this day, Indian Wells has not. In every city and county where there is a redevelopment agency, the same statutes apply, and unless they have complied with their conditions, then we cannot be recipients of their failure to build in their community," Montenegro said. Coachella did not want a hand out from their tanned and blow-dried neighbor.

The public nature of the debate annoyed reclusive Indian Wells. With the defeat, the $1.5 million will be added to the $13 million that will be used to build a 122-unit low-income senior complex "which is appropriate for the community because most of the community is seniors."[32]

SERENITY COMETH

Redevelopment agencies continue to pose an interesting dilemma in California. Reforms since Indian Wells formed its redevelopment agency

---

[30]Interview, April 14, 2000.
[31]Interview, April 11, 2000.
[32]Interview, April 14, 2000.

in 1983 have tightened the definition of blight and development of open space. Statutory changes make it harder for redevelopment agencies to neglect their housing requirement. And despite their shortcomings, redevelopment agencies have done much to improve the quality of life in many cities and built tens of thousands of low-income housing units for our neediest citizens.

For the residents in Coachella Valley, the 17-year saga has ended. After this last attempt at transfer, Indian Wells allowed its redevelopment agency to expire. On March 7, 2000, residents of Indian Wells approved, in a largely perfunctory vote, the construction of the senior housing that will rival only their first senior complex in terms of expense.[33] Indian Wells is currently attempting to annex a championship quality tennis complex—one of the country's largest—on land adjacent to the city.

Mayor Montenegro is building 576 new homes for very low-income residents. Recently, President Bill Clinton's Secretary of Housing and Urban Development, Andrew Cuomo, visited Coachella to applaud its low-income housing efforts and announce an $800,000 grant for farmworker housing. City Councilman Juan DeLara is still fighting to overturn the one point victory of Rosanna Contreras. He claims his mother couldn't vote because of a technical error and wants to overturn the election.

---

[33]*Palm Springs Desert Sun*, March 8, 2000.

Case 11

INTRODUCTION

At the outset, map out the problem from a policy standpoint. Equality is a principle not cherished in every human activity; but is there anyone who would argue today that justice should not be administered equally? Is it therefore surprising that the principle of state funding of trial courts should present so many problems at the policy level? What factors may have contributed to improving the prospects of passage?

The Latin motto symbolizing the federalism that is a distinctive feature of our national government is *E pluribus unum*—meaning from many (emerges) one. In the case *With Justice for All,* we encounter a situation in which there are many different counties (rather than states), each maintaining its own system of trial courts theoretically in furtherance of one single justice system for California. But does one in fact receive the same opportunities for fair proceedings in each of the 58 counties? Far from it, as the facts disclose. Successfully making one from many is not just a quantitative problem; it is qualitative as well.

What are the various factors that contributed to very different systems of justice in the different counties? What made the difference more pronounced in recent times than in former years? Is equal justice under the law taken too literally in the case? Are not there always going to be social, economic, cultural, and attitudinal differences among the different regions and municipal entities that comprise the state? Can the state so much more equitably distribute resources that these differences will suddenly vanish? What of the difficulty of encouraging those counties that were fairly well off to help make the new system work?

Writing, and even enacting, a law with noble goals such as equal justice may present difficulties, but what about implementing it? If room is left for a great deal of interpretation, and less uniformity of application, how do you assure consistent standards? What if counties use their allocated resources with vastly different levels of efficiency and even divert them for collateral or unintended purposes? How, in the implementation, do you provide for policing? In the case, what kind of organization provided the oversight before and after enactment of the law? How did it change to accommodate its new challenges? With what success?

On the other hand, if the law is too tightly written, you soon discover, in the implementation that one size does not fit all. Draw on your own experience: recall from your early math days that adding equals to unequals merely preserves inequality at a higher level. Thus, a law that distributes resources equally to all counties on, for example, a capitation basis certainly will not do the job.

Even if some flexibility of implementation is preserved, the problem remains complex. How do you formulate a system for allocating resources to a diverse group of public entities that fairly redresses legitimate inequalities, but not those that are a product of lack of effort or concern? How do you get these entities to overcome the inertia of history—to think differently, to change priorities, to rearrange relationships and to accept oversight? How successful were the chief actors in the case? How did they critique their own efforts? Which did you feel were most insightful? What might you have done differently? How do you rate the prospects of success? How would you measure success?

Trial Court Funding: With Justice for All

Research and original writing by Judicial Fellows Jeffrey Cuneo, Gary Flores, Jorge Jackson, Henry Oh, and Melissa Rodgers

INTRODUCTION

On September 13, 1997, the Lockyer-Isenberg Trial Court Funding Act was signed into law by Governor Pete Wilson. Prior to that time California's trial courts were a shambles notwithstanding incrementally successful efforts to address the situation. The people and forces responsible for the takeover of trial court funding by the state were many; this case spotlights a few. Policy success motivated some of the key actors to tell their stories. Candor compelled them to point out that the possibility of failure in implementation still looms. Indeed, officials in some of California's counties wish state takeover had never happened.

VIEWS OF THE DILEMMA

Rubin Lopez' official title was legislative representative[1] for the California State Association of Counties. But his role as negotiator on behalf of California's 58 counties as part of the task force convened by the governor's Department of Finance required that he wear two hats at the bargaining table. On some issues, in order to secure needed leverage, he had to persuade others that the counties, having so many interests in common, were tightly unified. As a solution began to crystallize, he had to get those same policy architects to appreciate the enormous differences among that same group of counties.

---

[1] A term used synonymously with the more familiar word "lobbyist."

Proposition 13[2] had severely limited counties' ability to raise their own revenues, he explained. At first, when the state provided a backfill for lost revenues, the strain was bearable. A long recession prevented that questionable arrangement from continuing. When Proposition 98 passed, locking up 40 percent of the budget for education,[3] the state essentially diverted most of the county revenues supplied by the state to the schools. The counties, and the programs they administered, were left in harm's way. One of the programs imposed on the counties was the responsibility to maintain "their" trial courts, the point of entry to the justice system for many.

With virtually no control over income, the counties remained financially responsible for court functions over which they had no control. When they tried to limit court costs, the courts cautioned them that interference with the discharge of judicial responsibilities violated the separation of powers provisions of the state and federal constitutions.

If the courts concluded the shortage of funds forced them to deny due process to people, noted Pedro Reyes, chief budget program analyst for the DOF, judges in some counties were contending they had the power to remedy the situation by appropriating funds from the county budget for court use. "Rational budgeting by the affected counties became impossible" said Reyes. "Supervisors' priorities for the use of limited funds were being ignored." Soon they would come to the state, he feared, as their programs began collapsing. Addressing the problem in any fashion would require data on how much the counties were spending on their trial courts; but "we did not know —at least there was no accurate data—what was being spent."

One motivation for poor record keeping seemed obvious. Why should they want to subject themselves to criticism from the courts for spending too little, and tax groups for spending too much? Foggy records allowed the counties the option to shift blame for their predicament not only to the state, but to the judiciary. Tax-concerned citizens already suspected the courts were living it up at their expense. Program-dependent citizens were equally ready to believe the courts were not taking their fair share of the cuts inflicted on programs for the poor.

---

[2]The initiative measure, passed by the people in 1976, severely curtailed the property tax revenues relied on mainly by local governments.

[3]Proposition 98 passed in 1978; the precise formula is more complex than a flat 40 percent.

According to Anthony Williams, legislative advocate[4] for the Judicial Council—a state body charged with administrative coordination of the courts—the state level judiciary had a concern that was different from that of the local trial courts. Staffing the Judicial Council was the job of the Administrative Office of the Courts. Its director pointed out that while local judges focused on due process needs, the state judiciary had a constitutional principle to protect—equal protection under the law. As Williams put it, "Whether you live in Los Angeles or tiny Alpine County, you should get the same level of justice."

The problem is that legal theory and logic run smack into historical reality. "The trial courts had developed as creatures of the different counties and continued to be treated that way, even though they were adjudicating state law," says Williams. Many people find security in the status quo even after its logic has been successfully challenged. Many more continue to rally to the banner of local control, ready to do instant battle against proposals to empower additional layers of government distant from the people.

Craig Cornett, director of criminal justice and state administration in the bipartisan and highly regarded Legislative Analyst's Office, believes, "People can understand the need for equal treatment throughout the state. However, when 58 frustrated counties with different ideas, resources, needs and cultures have responsibility for keeping the courts going, it won't happen. Even if all the counties agreed with the objective of equal access, no single county has the power to make it happen. Only the state does."

Surprisingly, for a local government representative, Lopez agrees with both state-level entities—the AOC and the LAO. "This is just not an area where the counties cherish their freedom and independence," he says. "They don't have the money, and they don't have the control they would need to make it work. They are never sure what their ultimate costs will be. They, and the local courts in each county, have different priorities than other counties and their courts. This is the reality even without the conflicts between a county and its courts within the county. It is why the counties and CSAC have long supported state takeover of trial court funding."

Another complicating factor is that counties and courts have had to struggle with very different timetables. While the counties were preparing their budgets, the courts might be out seeking funding from the state, then

---

[4]Another term used synonymously with the more familiar word "lobbyist."

coming back to the counties to meet the rest of their poorly documented needs—taking two bites at the apple. The resulting uncertainty made for lackadaisical record keeping, which made the full extent of the problem impossible to measure.

Although some narrow portion of the public was severely impacted by these conditions, the victim class was not large or stable enough to emerge as a political force. The lack of public attention was matched by a lack of leadership. Why would a politically accountable leader tackle an immensely difficult problem for which there would be few, if any, political rewards? What changes in circumstances were necessary to even justify a glimmer of hope that a solution was feasible?

LEADERSHIP QUEST

One morning in 1989, Phil Isenberg—Assemblymember, former mayor, and once chief consultant to the Assembly Ways and Means Committee—had just been seated at a local Sacramento restaurant. He was awaiting the arrival of Jim Ford, presiding judge of the Sacramento Superior Courts. When breakfast turned into business, Ford instituted a discussion of problems related to the effectiveness of the Judicial Council.

Although impressed by the magnitude of the problems related, and slated to become chair of the Assembly Judiciary Committee, Isenberg was not eager to involve himself. First, he recognized at once that increased state involvement in the administration, and possible funding, of the local[5] trial courts was in the MEGO (i.e., my eyes glaze over) category. Second, legislators, in their home districts, were beaten up regularly for imposing unfunded mandates on local government, and the financial bind of the state might well make this one. Third, Isenberg recognized that in order to do his best work, he would need to muster personal enthusiasm beyond what he then possessed about so seemingly mundane a subject.

Slightly intrigued nonetheless, Isenberg began to contemplate policy implications that were initially concealed by the immense detail. He realized that what was really at stake was the administration of justice in the largest state in the Union—including constitutional responsibilities of

---

[5]Traditionally, trial courts in California were recognized as local, notwithstanding state constitutional requirements and that it was largely state law they were construing.

access, evenhandedness, and quality. But where would the political impetus come from? How could one subdue the fears, suspicions, and inertia of the key actors, whose votes and support he would need, not to mention overcoming their diverse parochial allegiances? What of the dangers of an independent and co-equal third branch of government being turned into just another administrative agency? And yet, did he come all this way to tackle small or easy problems?

Responding to these concerns, Isenberg would become, along with Senator Lockyer[6] later in the game, the foremost legislative figure in the re-ordering of California's judicial system.

"HUMPTY DUMPTY" ON THE MEND

In the executive branch of California government, among the numerous agencies in the line authority of the governor, the Department of Finance is unquestionably the governor's powerful right arm.

According to Diane Cummins, assistant director of DOF, everyone participating conceptually "shared the same goal of wanting to see the courts adequately funded so that they were open and accessible." Beyond that, the governor expressed concern about efficiencies (e.g., the coordinated automation of information) needed to hold down costs. He asked DOF to see if a framework for politically acceptable legislation could be found in time for the Governor's unveiling of his 1996-97 budget.

DOF director, Russ Gould, injected the additional objective of providing some major long-term fiscal relief for counties. Their budgets, in many cases, had been reduced to rubble since 1992-93, when a four-month late budget triggered a huge shift of revenues away from the counties and to the schools—the end of the state's Proposition 13 backfill. Blaming the governor and the legislature, the counties (and soon those who depended on them) were devastated. The governor wanted to re-establish good relations with the counties, but keeping him on board required that it be done in a way the governor considered responsible, and as was widely

---

[6]Former Senate Judiciary Chair, then Senate President Pro Tempore, and now State Attorney General.

known, politically acceptable to him.[7] The TCF proposal seemed to fit the bill. Gould asked Cummings and two others to put together a task force consisting of the three main parties—the counties, the courts, and the administration. Its work was to be under wraps.

Beyond providing a more rational approach, the new state funds helped address the fiscal problems of the counties and released them from an open-ended burden they should never have had. Though it involved the sensitive issue of criminal justice, the LAO's Craig Cornett doubted the counties would regard it as another power grab by the state, because the courts were a much larger thorn in their sides. "They felt like the courts were holding them hostage," he says. Besides, the authority the counties were giving up was purely illusory. They never had it in the first place.

As for acceptance by the courts, the LAO believed that many of the courts, particularly in the poorer and smaller counties, could see that their needs would be better met by an entity with a large general fund than by the financially strapped counties.

Then there was the legislature. Surely, some reasoned, state lawmakers would see it as a perfect fit. They would provide the counties with relief that was obviously needed, while relieving themselves of the exasperating bifurcated system of partial-state and partial-local funding of the trial courts.

DOF's specialist in the area, Pedro Reyes, was less sanguine. There was a subtlety that was being missed. Achieving the desired efficiencies was not enough. If serious monies were to be transferred to the counties, the lawmakers would demand a visible method of demonstrating accountability—one that would include continuing scrutiny and periodic reporting from the overseers.

In fact, the LAO's advice to the legislature had been exactly that. It cautioned against providing unfettered monies raised by state policymakers (who paid the political price for doing so) to local officials (who did not feel the same pressure to be sure that the funds were spent wisely). Earmarking the funds for the trial courts in the counties was not enough. State oversight procedures for holding courts accountable would need to be part of the legislation before legislators should get on board. The LAO

---

[7]It meant not handing "discretionary" money over to the counties that could be used to satisfy public employee unions with whom he had an ongoing battle before and during his terms as governor.

recommended that the Judicial Council, a state-level body with responsibility, but not the means, to oversee the efficiency of court operations was the entity best positioned to protect state interests.

Says Williams of the tactical role of the Judicial Council: "As far as leadership, one notable part of all this was the very active role played by the Supreme Court's Chief Justice Ronald George. He was new on the scene but waded right in to help get votes, something that would have made the former Chief Justice somewhat uncomfortable."

Cummings had a somewhat different slant: The complaint that this was a power grab by Bill Vickrey and the Chief Justice popped up again and again. Later, they, and others like legislative leaders of both parties, had to go around the state to allay the fears of judges.

Summing it up from the vantage point of DOF, Diane Cummins noted a number of problems that might have been dealt with better, but she believes the result was absolutely correct from a policy standpoint. "The old county-centered bifurcated system decimated the county budget process," she says.

> It became piecemeal and irrational. There were timing conflicts, information vacuums, last minute changes and a number of things that made for weak planning and poor fiscal dependability. The counties were not getting adequate funds from the state and then the courts came after their share. Even with the power to hold the counties hostage and order them to provide what they deemed essential, the courts were not necessarily funded at an adequate level either. It was partly the recession, but also sentencing laws like three strikes increased the workload and backlogs. In the end no one got all that he or she wanted and that's a good sign. What is more important, *no one* lost; everyone gained. The timing was right, the political climate was right, the kind of leaders and staff we needed were there, and so it happened.

ROUGH AT THE EDGES?

Still, there were a number of loose ends, some anticipated, some not. Amidst the general euphoria, it was Pedro Reyes, again, who sounded a caution: "You would think that the really hard problems had been worked out in the legislation after all we went through. It seemed to satisfy almost everyone with a major stake in the outcome. But it did not happen; the details of implementation were every bit as tough. The varying degrees of sophistication among the counties meant we had to provide accounting information and it had to be in computer-friendly format. CSAC and the AOC have been setting up programs that are the equivalent of schools for local officials."

While that could be anticipated, Anthony Williams conceded some surprises: "We recognized there could not be a pure system of state trial court funding, but we thought that there would be a clear line between state and local responsibilities—that the state would assume responsibility for those costs necessary for the operation of the courts using our model of what constitutes a well-functioning system, but not for all court-related costs. The state would fund the judges, their staff, and other directly related entities without which our model system would not work. It would not fund the costs of district attorneys, public defenders, or their offices. We assumed it would be easy to figure out, but it wasn't.

"There were assumptions about how much it costs to run courts, how much counties had been contributing, and how much we could generate in fees. But how could we arrive at dependable judgments when they rested on the very information that had not been provided before trial court funding?

"Labor issues had not been resolved. Were court employees to be treated as county or as state employees? Was there to be collective bargaining? It was one of the things that had torpedoed previous legislation so we had agreed to postpone it. We set up a task force to develop a compromise. Who would pay for new facilities or upgrading or repairs? We created a task force to deal with that issue. Was there to be a *cap* on the counties' contributions to whatever their portion turned out to be? Lockyer in the end game imposed a pretty tight cap.

To secure the needed number of votes in the Legislature, the problems of the 20 or so smaller counties would have to be dealt with —they didn't have the resources to comply with substantial contributions, or even with extensive survey and reporting requirements. Some trial court judges, in counties that had been fairly well off, especially Los Angeles, complained about losing their power to big brother. They felt they had lost the ability to see a need, go down the street, and sit down with a longtime colleague to reach an agreement."

"After the first try failed," recalls Cummings, "remarkably, by sheer force of personality, we kept the coalition together. But, in doing so, we did not update the base year we used and it became unnecessarily contentious when complaints arose from those who would have fared better had we updated. It created some embarrassing anomalies."

> Then there was the aging principle—when some proposal sits in this building (the Capitol) for a long time, it becomes exposed, people pick at it, and some coalescing of the opposition occurs. Who knows whether this factor was avoidable? There were some things we simply did not know about, like *fees* that were being charged and where the money went when the counties got them. How vigorously the counties pursued fees depended on program incentives. If the state did not pick up uncovered costs, as in the case of the courts, they pushed hard.

Unexpectedly, he says, "A San Diego Superior Court case came down during our negotiations that hit us hard. It exempted superior courts from having to bargain over noneconomic labor issues. It ignited the collective bargaining controversy in a way that seemed irreconcilable. It was one of the most contentious issues; it involved employees, judges, court reporters, interpreters, and of course judges and counties."

IMPLEMENTATION

Recognizing some of the problems of implementation, Diane Cummins points out,

> Full implementation won't occur until the task forces we created, for issues we had to defer politically, come in with their recommendations. Judges aren't budget experts, and it will take time for them to learn to keep books, and in some cases realize they will have to before they receive their money.
>
> We underestimated the immensity of the change, the complexity involved, the difficulty with getting good data, the number of different roles and responsibilities, the size of the differences among counties, and the number of things going on that we simply did not know about; but we wound up with a fair and rational system, we got fiscal relief for the counties, and kept our coalition together despite very different perspectives. I hope that they adopt our approach in solving the problems remaining at the local level.

Adds Pedro Reyes, "We are talking about a team that represents all the affected parties, can fairly mediate differences, and can determine what fixes are needed. Both anticipated and unanticipated problems will continue to arise and need to be identified at the earliest possible time."

Adds Rubin Lopez, "The biggest fear is that someone will say we are all done and people will wash their hands and walk away. This is an ongoing process that will take at least 5-6 years. It took New York ten."

A VIEW FROM THE TOWER

Kiri Torre, director of Trial Court Services, a division within the AOC, agreed that trial court funding was a smashing policy success. "Nonetheless," she adds, "for the most part (before AB 233's enactment) the judges had a direct, usually beneficial, one-on-one relationship with county administrators and supervisors." For them, the new budget process, headed by a State Trial Court Budget Commission governed by state policy goals—the price of systemization—was "a serious loss of local autonomy." Indeed, they are the subject of surveys, that are the primary means for accounting for their requests for state funding allocations by the AOC. "They must justify their requests with workload data and other quantifiable measures . . . in greater detail [than before]."

"AOC," says Toore, "is doing everything within its power to make the experience less burdensome and easier on the courts. However, getting the courts to exercise budget discipline when, for so many years they did not have to, may be a continuing problem. While there is some lack of coordination among divisions in the AOC itself, causing some overlap in the information requested, it is getting better. It is doing everything in its power to make the experience less burdensome. As an agency, the AOC is evolving, changing the way it does business in order to meet the new demands placed upon it."

SOME VIEWS FROM BELOW—LOS COLOSSUS COUNTY[8]

Los Colossus, one of the larger counties in California, is made up of several incorporated cities ranging from urban to rural. Prior to state trial court funding, the county was the main source of money for court

---

[8]Fictitious names are used for the counties and their personnel "to protect the innocent."

functions. Economic problems plagued the courts constantly due to the inflexibility of the Los Colossus budget, which included funding for basic services that could not be eliminated and politically resisted reductions. The courts felt they would soon not even be able to conduct their business if left at the mercy of the county's budget. For the courts, state funding was a much-needed alternative, but one they viewed with some reservations. Especially for court administrators and other staff, it presented some harsh realities.

Management analyst Kiki Shepp has a broad perspective on the effects. Formerly executive officer of the Los Colossus courts, Kiki enjoyed a close relationship with the supervisors. She always felt comfortable going to the board if more money was needed. Los Colossus, she says, was a generous county, sympathetic to labor needs: "When the initial discussion of state funding began, it was positive. Courts would have state money and the county would no longer have the burden of funding them."

> Since its implementation, some extremely difficult issues for court personnel have arisen. Who controls how the money is spent, the courts or the state? Who can demand information, how much and what kind? Concealed within the promise of state funding, was the tremendous power given to the Administrative Office of the Courts and the Judicial Council. They have *de facto* authority over the courts. The AOC has generated administrative headaches for all the courts in the form of surveys. It is no exaggeration to say that the amount of administrative work for myself and others has increased ten fold.

Kiki feels that the AOC is "disorganized and confused." According to her, "The AOC does not know what information it needs to discharge its administrative operations. Even the quality of work is poor." Kiki suggests with some bitterness that its agents "step back and learn what a budget is, and how items should be accounted for. They should seek assistance from the Department of Finance, which can provide a management system for the truckloads of information they are gathering. Then maybe they can avoid starting from scratch every time they need court information."

Kiki's impression of the AOC is that it is "marred by internal struggles, and that this has caused them not to deal forthrightly with the courts." The major stakeholders in court funding, according to Kiki, are judges, court administrators, labor unions, and community members.

Judges will not be able to leverage their friendships with supervisors, and they are unclear about just what is required of them. Administrators are not in position to provide them with strategic advice. Labor unions will have a much more difficult time negotiating at the state level. The communities that make up Los Colossus County risk losing local court programs like marital and custody mediation, drug dependency, and foreign language interpreters because the state will not understand their importance in different areas.

Don Beck, a management analyst who worked for the AOC at one time, offers another perspective. His view of state funding seems influenced by the AOC and is more optimistic than Kiki's. On the negative side he fears that the courts may be following the same path that public school funding has taken: "State funding of courts may result in a local disconnect that diminishes support for them."

His optimism stems from a different scenario. He sees the imposition of rational budgeting as "a means of getting more people involved, assuring good management and, over time, securing sympathetic views toward the courts. Positive involvement would be further enhanced if the Judicial Council supports keeping the courts open longer, even 24 hours." Fears that the courts will not have the same influence in the state political arena as they did with the counties can be allayed, he believes, by "adding regional representation to the membership of the Judicial Council. Increased representation by local officials would undo worries about the fairness of actions taken by a council that is appointed and not elected."

Don says, "The book is still being written" on the understandably difficult transition process. "It has been managed about as well as can be expected; at best court administration is a messy business. Examining its processes closely can only increase everyone's understanding." Don adds that everyone in Los Colossus County court is managing okay, and the transition "is no different than starting a new business. Looking for someone to blame only thwarts the process of change."

THE VIEW FROM MIDTERREY COUNTY

Midterrey County, despite expectations, has had a largely positive experience with TCF. Court staff paint a bleak picture of the courts' situation prior to TCF. Executive Officer June Moss says that the high, and growing, crime rate in the county meant that the courts have had a high level of demand for their services. However, the county did not provide a corresponding increase in funds. "We had costs we had no control over," Moss says. As a result, she says, Midterrey County courts did not have enough money to provide the level of services needed to dispense justice in a fair and timely manner.

Lucita Smith is a superior court management analyst. In the past, she says, the court was not able to meet the public's demand for service. One year the court had to lay off people due to lack of funds. "The last few years we have simply existed, fighting our fears of shrinking to nothing," she says. "More than a third of our staff are not permanent employees." Prior to TCF, the court had no funds to invest in new technology, robbing it of any opportunity to increase efficiency. It had no on-site storage space for files; people needing files had to wait two days for the court to retrieve them. Although these problems did not disappear overnight with the advent of TCF, the courts in Midterrey County "are much better funded under state trial court funding," says Smith.

> Additional staff have been hired. Our doors are open from 8:30 a.m. to 5.00 p.m., five days a week. Requests are being handled more efficiently over the phone. The courts have begun to engage in community outreach programs that Chief Justice George supports very strongly. State funding has allowed us to dig out from under our financial burdens and do some good things. It has allowed us to staff at a level consistent with the workload.

Even though the courts in Midterrey County have had a largely positive experience with TCF, they are not immune to problems. But Moss feels that unlike some courts in other counties that have been very vocally opposed to TCF, the courts in Midterrey County took the problems in stride. Moss knew the transition was not going to be easy. So it was no surprise to her when problems occurred. "The budget process keeps shifting and changing," she says. "AOC sends out survey after survey to the courts and each time it seems the requirements are different." That is what Moss finds most frustrating.

Maria Palacios, a clerk administrator in the Midterrey County courts, says court employees do not fully support TCF because they are confused. "We have had countless meetings about it; but I don't think you can fully understand it unless you deal with it daily." she observes. Moss acknowledged, "Trying to help the staff understand the changes was very difficult because I did not have all the answers myself."

The courts have also had to deal with a deteriorating relationship with their county. Palacios says, "TCF was like getting a divorce." Questions about who will get the toaster continue to plague the courts in their relationship with the county. Moss says Midterrey County owes the courts more than $1.5 million for court security, but the courts have yet to see the money.

"The main problem," Moss believes, "is that the county leadership tends to focus on how much money they are still spending on the courts after TCF, rather than looking at the money they are saving. Who gets hurt anyway? The same people the supervisors represent."

She feels that, unlike the county, "The AOC was there for us. We had cash flow problems that would have affected our ability to meet payroll, and the county told us it was our problem. The AOC stepped in and gave us the funds we needed to meet payroll." Contrary to what she had expected from a centralized, administrative agency, June found the AOC to be very responsive.

The one issue that drove leaders at every level of government to support TCF, says Moss, was the issue of consistency in the delivery of justice by courts throughout the state. She thinks that better economic times gave the state the resources to take on the issue, and the counties the incentive to support TCF to reduce otherwise uncontrollable costs.

Palacios scoffs at the notion that TCF is a ploy on the part of the AOC to grab more power. She finds it natural for AOC to take the lead in transforming the system. "Consistent justice is the AOC's role," she says. "It requires central administration. Although there are statewide priorities, the AOC is still giving us significant discretion." Palacios does not believe that TCF eroded the autonomy of the courts because "the reality is that prior to TCF, the county courts were paralyzed."

A FINAL VIEW FROM BELOW—MINIPINE COUNTY

Minipine County is the mostly rural home to 150,000 people with two small cities—population 10,000 and 30,000. The rest of the county is unincorporated. The county's low revenue base makes it heavily dependent on state and local government.

Karen Thompson is the principal administrative analyst in the county administrative office. Initially, she says, the county welcomed the concept of state trial court funding (TCF). But Minipine County had not understood that the funding would be limited to trial court operations as defined under Rule 8.10. The county has concerns about costs not included in the definition. "Now, for example, if grants become available to create new programs such as drug courts, who is responsible for providing matching funds or authorizing the grant?" Thompson asks. "If drug courts are alternatives to normal trial court operations, should the county play a role?"

From the county's perspective, the thorniest issues posed by TCF relate to indirect costs and personnel. "Technically," Thompson explains, "even though courts are responsible for their operation costs, court employees are still county employees. If a court doesn't have enough money for payroll, the county has to pay." Consequently, the county feels compelled to monitor the court budget. But Thompson says Minipine County has lost awareness of court operations. "Before trial court funding," she explains, "the courts invited me or I asked for a briefing. Not anymore." In addition, the county is held to Maintenance of Effort (MOE) funding figures, based on quarterly financial reports filed by the courts. Because the courts had included county indirect costs in their reporting, Minipine County must continue to pay these costs. On some level, Minipine County feels it may have been set up by the courts.

Thompson remembers that CSAC had been active for years trying to find a way to get fiscal relief for under funded counties. At one time, counties received block grants from the state, but the grants were reduced. She thinks the block grant system was more efficient than state trial court funding.

Reflecting on county-based funding, Thompson says: "Given where things stand today, courts were better off under that system because local administrators understood the needs of the courts. The courts probably thought they were disadvantaged," she continues, "but I doubt they think that anymore." Now, Thompson feels that the courts continue to be underfunded. The court submits budget requests that the AOC supports, but funding is not forthcoming. She does not know where to locate the problem—perhaps in the Judicial Council, or in the legislature. She is suspicious of the AOC, whose ongoing requests for information disrupt court operations. "So often we hear from local court staff scrambling to complete a survey or a data request," she says. "There are times when I wonder whether the people at the AOC know the impact of their requests. Do they think about what they need and then ask specific enough questions?" The counties must also respond to surveys. Minipine County is awaiting a definitive decision on the status of trial court employees. The Employee and Facilities task forces, which include representatives from the counties and the judiciary, are still gathering information. Thompson says that Minipine County has no real power in the process. "We just help by completing surveys," she says.

During the transition to TCF, working with the AOC has proved difficult. "Depending on whom you talk to, you get inconsistent answers," Thompson says. "Sometimes they don't return our phone calls at all." Although the AOC has made itself available to clarify instructions, Minipine County has not felt supported. "We had a statewide, all-county briefing," she continues. "The most common answer to our questions was, 'That's a good question; we're still working on it,' or, 'You'll have to work that out at the local level.'" Consequently, the counties launched a series of meetings to share notes.

Thompson does not believe Minipine County has lost any power with the TCF process. But she fears courts will not receive the resources they need and that the state will not recognize the needs of the smallest counties. She worries that Minipine County's courts will have trouble competing with the large jurisdictions.

Court Executive Officer Alan Woods shares her concern. "It was a very important opportunity to upgrade the level of service and equipment of underfunded courts," he says. He believes deeply in the concept of state funding and is dismayed by its implementation. Mostly, he attributes the problems with TCF to lack of planning and misinformation. He says the state lacked data when it decided to enact the funding legislation. As a result, cost savings and total costs were misrepresented. Woods believes AOC did not fully understand the costs it would incur as a result of having to administer trial court funding statewide. Meanwhile, hidden costs have emerged at the county level. For instance, in the past, counties provided services for which they billed only partly, if at all. Thus these costs were never reflected in the court budget and were excluded from the baseline budget that courts must now use for operations.

The budget cycle is a nightmare for Minipine County's courts. Woods says, "We are always behind." Staff needs always arise at the wrong part of the budget cycle. The Department of Finance bases most budget changes on documented workload increases. This approach does not cover fee increases for court-appointed counsel or cost of living increases. Woods thinks that the Trial Court Budget Commission should first and foremost reevaluate the courts' baseline budget. However, he says, "It is easier to fight about Y2K or new programs than to go back to the baseline. The Department of Finance and the legislature don't want to hear about baseline issues. And, for political reasons, the Judicial Council doesn't want to push too hard." Moreover, the budget process does not rely on articulated standards (for example, for levels of staffing or equipment) and uses statewide average measures that underestimate the needs of smaller counties. As Woods noted in a 1998 letter to the AOC, "There is a significant dichotomy between the AOC's numbers . . . and our on-the-ground experience."

One problem is that trial court costs are now viewed from a statewide perspective, "When the AOC addresses the issues of the trial courts," says Woods, "it must do so statewide. It must create a macro-picture out of 58 micro-pictures. Some of the local nuances are lost." For example, for two years in a row Minipine County's courts have unsuccessfully requested funding for several new court-reporter positions. "No degree of planning will ensure that we get this funding," says Woods. Describing the difficulties of dealing with the Legislature, he says political gamesmanship eliminated the Court Modernization Fund, thereby denying courts funding to become Y2K compliant. "But we cannot leave the Y2K problem unaddressed," he says. "So we end up with a budget deficit."

Woods fumes over the bureaucratic mindset—"Don't ever address an issue until you are forced to do so," This leaves the system no time for anything except handling crises as they arise. "The court was probably better off with the old system," he says. "It was more informal, more flexible, and more timely. We got what we needed." He believes counties are the primary beneficiaries of the new legislation, although they have lost final control over court operations. By contrast, individual trial courts have lost control of the budget process and management decision making without any financial rewards. The courts must now turn to the AOC to find out what their budget is, and the AOC delays in sending out the results of its (public) budget meetings. The red tape frustrates Alan Woods. "If I don't know what my budget is, I can't do my job," he says. "All decisions critical to the issues I face are in the hands of people over whom I have no influence."

Woods notes that large counties have retained power. He attributes this to the structure of the Judicial Council and its advisory committees. The important advisory committees do not include representatives from courts with fewer than five judicial officers. "Smaller courts, whether well-funded or not, do not have the capacity to participate in statewide decision-making bodies," he says. "We don't have the resources to volunteer our time. It would be better if the AOC had staff who worked in small trial courts and could understand the impact of limited resources on the smaller courts." He says current procedures have been developed without any understanding of the Minipine Courts' inability to respond. "The AOC has paid lip-service to the notion of consulting trial court executives and presiding judges, but while the trial courts wanted one process, the AOC chose another that was easier to manage. Los Angeles sent a letter to the TCBC, requesting that the budget process include all courts; instead, the AOC consulted with the Judicial Council's advisory committees, which are dominated by large courts." Woods fears, "We small counties will never catch up, and the larger counties that were progressive may be held back. We could lose innovation as a branch of government."

Case 12

INTRODUCTION

Why are public-private partnerships so difficult to sustain in the United States—even with California's progressive and dynamic private sector leading the experimental way? In many countries, like Japan, they are a mainstay. But when Stanford University and the University of California, San Francisco recently merged their medical centers in the interest of efficiency and improved patient care, the experiment was a short-lived failure.

In *91 Ways to Leave a Toll Road*, we find some insight into the risks involved. Private investors are willing to serve public objectives if there is a bottom line return on their investment. Public managers are willing to help provide a reasonable return so long as it is compatible with their goal of providing needed service. Both would agree that the most efficient ways to reach their goals are best. But what if profit and the provision of optimum service conflict? Is that what occurred here? How would you describe the conflict?

It is sometimes said that ambiguity lubricates the passage of controversial legislation. What was the great ambiguity here that permitted a divergence of public and private goals? Should the incompatible needs have been anticipated from the outset? Was anyone to blame? Who?

When the toll road idea was conceived as a solution to heavy traffic and no money, did the governor and the legislature feel they had much choice? Should public agencies and public representatives expect that what makes good policy in one environment will be regarded as good policy in another?

Note Lockyer's fear as a liberal state senator that *this toll road might be a private investor ripoff*. Compare that with Attorney General Lockyer's much later observation that *even with their advantages, those investors were unable to make a profit*.

Note State Senator Seymour's conservative philosophy that *the private sector can do it better*. Compare that with conservative Assemblyman McClintock's position that *we should not grant private-sector monopolies*.

Was it wrong for private investors to try to salvage their position by seeking public assistance (tax-exempt bonds) to offset Caltrans' alleged broken promises not to compete? Although designed to improve traffic in the public interest, is it not clear Caltrans violated its part of the bargain to not compete? If you had been Caltrans director, would you have approved conversion to a nonprofit? Was any *hanky panky* going on? Or was it a case of transforming structures to accommodate changed circumstances and expectations?

Public-Private Partners:
91 Ways to Leave a Toll Road

Research and original writing by Senate Fellow Carla C. Dane

A BIT OF HISTORY

Since the beginning of organized travel, private citizens who control thoroughfares have charged for their use. The fee, or toll, might compensate investors for construction or maintenance of a road, a canal, or a ferry. The size of the toll might be governed by what the appropriate regulatory agency or utility law deems reasonable. Or it might simply be raised to reflect whatever the traffic will bear, a common expression whose origins are, in this context, obvious.

Thoroughfares built to promote commerce or the movement of troops might require an investment that is either too large or too risky for an individual. The public treasury might also be tapped to build a highway for the king or for a government agency. Although user fees could be imposed in each case, qualified users might not have to pay anything except at tax time.

Residents of the Eastern United States, long accustomed to paying tolls, call their modern highways turnpikes and extract users' fees at strategically situated tollbooths. When Californians built bridges to span northern water crossings, they adopted a toll system. As early as 1923, when their love affair with the automobile began, Californians experimented with a tax on gasoline *exclusively* to pay for roads. That convenient and widely accepted precedent was used when Californians contemplated a modern highway system to cope with the astonishing growth that characterized the second half of the twentieth century. Marketed as *free*ways rather than turnpikes, the new highway system (notwithstanding federal subsidies) was far from free—state costs were included in the price paid for gasoline. At least the annoyance of frequent stops to pay tolls was eliminated.

It was a harmonious arrangement—the more people drove, the more their freeways improved, and more and better freeways attracted more cars. Suddenly, as in a pyramid scheme, breakdowns began to slow the momentum of this beloved perpetual motion machine. The fashionable solution—the governor and the California Department of Transportation (Caltrans) might have called it unavoidable—was privatization. And the obvious choice was a variation on an old theme—the toll road.

LIMITS TO GROWTH

The Department of Transportation's ambitious plans to expand California's highway system to accommodate future growth came to a halt in the 1970s. After the election of environmentalist Governor Jerry Brown in 1974, Caltrans postponed the construction of a substantial portion of the state's highway segments in response to arguments that the improvements promoted sprawl, smog, and excessive energy use. The few projects undertaken were downsized to preclude expansion as the population grew. Not only was there a failure to complete the system as originally envisioned, but scarcely noticed, deterioration set in.

To compound the problem, antitax sentiment swept through California. In 1978, voters approved Proposition 13 limiting state and local property tax revenues. A few years later, voters approved the Gann cap on state spending. Energy shortages and increased gasoline costs reduced state revenues further. Finally, when Democrats in the legislature pushed for a gas tax hike in 1987, Governor Deukmejian and conservative Republican legislators insisted the voters approve it. Californians defeated the measure, though the results could not be announced until early July, when the absentee ballots had been counted, due to the closeness of the race.[1]

There were cost problems as well. The dense development encouraged by freeways made land near them scarce and more expensive—limiting the construction of new freeways or more lanes. Urban sprawl forced

---

[1] Jose A. Gomez-Ibanez and John R. Meyer, "Private Toll Roads in the United States and the Early Experience of Virginia and California," (U.S. Department of Transportation Final Report, John F. Kennedy School of Government, Harvard University, December 1, 1991), 69.

homeowners to live further away from their jobs, adding to the number of commuters on the freeways. People and cars were increasing faster than freeways could be built to accommodate them. With no effective mass transit alternatives, traffic began to crawl at a snail's pace. Some freeways were virtually parking lots. Then, California entered a lengthy recession.

"EVERYTHING OLD IS NEW AGAIN"

In 1989, the state was looking for answers. Setting aside new routes, California needed more than $100 billion to expand and improve existing routes. Private toll roads had been introduced in a number of states with varying success. Why not in California? "Our choice is simple," said Carl Williams, the assistant director of Caltrans. "We either find a way to fill our funding gap with private capital, or we do not build these projects at all. Doing nothing about all the unmet needs out there is unacceptable politically and morally."[2] "The private sector had said they could do it cheaper and better," noted Williams, "And we want to say to them, okay, put up or shut up."[3]

Beset with revenue deficiencies for needed infrastructure, the California legislature embarked on a bold experiment with the private sector. In January 1989, Assemblyman Bill Baker of Danville introduced Assembly Bill 680. He proposed to allow the state to grant four franchises to private firms interested in building and operating toll roads. The private investments would preclude the need for extracting tax revenues from the public. Four factors made AB 680 especially appealing:

- It would not legalize privately owned toll roads. Once construction was complete, the developer would transfer ownership to the state.
- The private firm would bear all construction and maintenance costs. It could lease the facility for up to 35 years, after which it would revert unencumbered to the state.
- Although the lessee could recover costs, only reasonable profits were permitted.
- The projects would have to relieve congestion.

---

[2] William G. Rheinhardt, "Kiewet Moves SR 91 Financing to Closure Launching a New Era in U.S. Toll Roads," *Public Works Financing* 65 (July/August 1993): 7.

[3] Jose A. Gomez-Ibanez and John R. Meyer, 74.

In theory, the state would obtain maximum benefit with minimal risk. AB 680 moved easily through the Senate and Assembly, and Governor Deukmejian signed it into law on July 10.

"When you looked … at the price the Republicans were demanding in order to put $20 billion into a deteriorating transportation system, it seemed to be a reasonable deal," said Assembly Transportation Committee Chairman Richard Katz.[4]

Over 600 firms contacted Caltrans to express interest in bidding for the opportunity to build a franchise roadway. Roy Nagy of Caltrans' Office of Public/Private Partnerships, who worked closely with Carl Williams, was completely open in his pitch to private contractors. "You have to pay for everything," he told them. "Your have all the design costs, environmental costs, construction costs. Just before it's open, you have to deed it back to the state. The state will lease it back to you for a maximum of 35 years. When we issue you the 35-year lease, you're responsible to pay for all maintenance and police services. We're going to put a ceiling on how much you can make, but there is no floor to how much you can lose."

"All the risk was on the private sector, and amazingly they wanted to participate," said Nagy, "They said it sounds good to us." The most important aspect of the negotiation process for Nagy was to make it clear to the private sector that, "This wasn't government as usual." Every Caltrans district director knew the technical details of the program and worked one-on-one with competing firms to reduce the wait time to consider each proposal.

Between 1980 and 1990, the eight-lanes of the Riverside Freeway experienced a traffic growth rate of 8.4 percent per year. It currently carries more than 250,000 vehicles per day. This will increase to 330,000 to 400,000 vehicles per day in less than 10 years.[5] "This is one of the worst freeways and the worst congestion in the state of California," said Assemblyman Rod Pacheco. "And it is only going to double in the next 15 years because of our population. It takes 30 minutes in one stretch of road to go a mile and a half. It takes a great deal more than that on your psyche

---

[4]Virginia Ellis, "Toll Road Projects Lose Momentum," *Los Angeles Times*, February 8, 2000.

[5]California Private Transportation Company, "The 91 Express Lanes: A Fast, Safe, Reliable Alternative to Gridlock," (Senate Transportation Committee Binder), 1.

when you are driving that freeway every morning."[6] The dramatic increase is a direct effect of the exponential growth of affordable homes in Riverside and Eastern Orange County and the proliferation of jobs in Orange County.

In 1990, Caltrans offered one of the four projects to a private bidder—the California Private Transportation Company (CPTC), a consortium of Level 3 Communications, the Cofiroute Corporation (the California subsidiary of a French toll road operator), and Granite Construction Company. CPTC won the exclusive right to design, build, and operate four express lanes in the median of State Highway 91, the Riverside Freeway. The toll lanes would stretch 10 miles, with no entrance or exit along the way, using state right-of-way from the State 91/State 55 interchange in Orange County east to the Riverside/Orange County border.

A DISCOMFORTING AFTERTHOUGHT

In a letter to Caltrans Director Robert Best on September 28, 1990, Assemblyman Richard Katz expressed a prescient concern about potential problems with the implementation of AB 680. "In order to assure a toll revenue stream over a long-term period of time," wrote Katz, "it's my understanding the department intends to include provisions in the contracts which would guarantee that the state would not build facilities that would 'compete' with the toll roads over the duration of the agreement. . . . This arrangement could prohibit the state from building facilities to relieve future traffic that we can't even estimate at this time in corridors that link growing areas."

In other words, any capacity improvements along the general use lanes of 91 would reduce the number of vehicles using the toll facility, thus reducing its beneficial and tax-free contribution to the alleviation of congestion. Two weeks later Best assured Katz that Caltrans would work to prevent state and local entities from developing competing facilities. In fact, CPTC insisted on a "Non-Competition Provision," wherein Caltrans would be prohibited from funding and constructing almost any transportation project that would adversely affect the volume of traffic within the project. As Hulsizer explains, "Our parent company never would have

---

[6]Joint Hearing: Assembly Transportation Committee and Senate Transportation Committee: "State Route 91 Expressways," February 1, 2000.

invested in this project without some type of financial security."[7] Caltrans could still make improvements within the designated zone in the interests of safety. After all, the purpose of the exclusivity agreement was not to prevent Caltrans from making its roadway safer for those using it, but to avoid its attracting new customers. Besides, there was ample precedent for non-competition agreements both within and outside California.[8]

CHANGING LANES

On July 27, 1993, Governor Pete Wilson broke ground. The project would test congestion pricing, which charged a higher toll at peak travel times. Vehicles with three or more occupants could travel the facility at no cost. Fees would not be collected at tollbooths. CPTC had developed the technology for the FasTrak transponder—a four-inch square device mounted inside the windshield on the driver's side that charged a member's account. CPTC had tow trucks to remove cars that stalled in the lanes.

Before the toll road opened, the portion of westbound 91 in Riverside County adjacent to the toll road had four general-purpose lanes and two high-occupancy vehicle (HOV or carpool) lanes. In order to build the toll road within the median, the six westbound lanes were reduced to four at the Riverside County Line, and HOV cars had to weave into the smaller roadway. Caltrans and CPTC agreed on a gradual reduction for safety reasons. It meant giving up some significant nontoll road capacity and making life harder (albeit safer) for commuters. In response, the Riverside County Transportation Commission (RCTC) sued CPTC in May 1994. It claimed CPTC and Caltrans altered design plans without informing them and had failed to conduct an environmental review. A Superior Court judge essentially found RCTC's allegations without merit.

In December 1995, the $130 million toll road opened for business. The advantages seemed far-reaching. CPTC General Manager, Greg Hulsizer, said: "The commuters were offered an option they would not have had for

---

[7]Greg Hulsizer, telephone interview, March 9, 2000.

[8]The 14-mile toll road linking Dulles International Airport with Leesburg, Virginia almost went bankrupt and had to restructure its debt when improvements by the Virginia Department of Transportation to competing roads reduced its patronage. Toll corridors in southern California all have some sort of noncompetition clause in their operating agreements.

many years to come, the state got a road built with no tax dollars, and there are obvious environmental benefits."

In 1996 and 1997, despite the fact that income exceeded costs, debt service on the project produced enormous losses.[9] CPTC began charging car-poolers, motorcyclists, and persons with disabilities. A threatened lawsuit by RCTC was averted when CPTC voluntarily opened its financial records to prove the extent of its losses.

Other numbers showed the 91 Express Lanes were functioning well. In a joint 1997 study completed by Caltrans and the U.S. Department of Transportation, average weekday traffic in the toll lanes was approaching 30,000 vehicles per day—about 13 percent of the traffic on 91. The increased capacity from two new toll lanes in each direction reduced peak freeway congestion on 91. In the sixth months after the opening of the express lanes, the typical peak trip delay on the freeway fell from 30-40 minutes to less than 10 minutes. The study notes, "A year later, at the end of our observation period in June 1997, the P.M. peak trip delay had increased by about 5 minutes to the 12-13 minute range, reflecting both time shifts in travel demand and the effect of the long-term traffic growth trend."[10]

The study suggested that traffic using the toll facility and the vehicles using the general purpose lanes of the 91 Freeway had reached an equilibrium—that the toll road had not increased traffic on the route, but rather had reduced congestion, which was its intended purpose. Peak travel tolls increased from $2.50 in December 1995, $2.75 in January 1997, and $3.20 by April 1998—all without a significant downturn in ridership.

AMBIGUITY COMES HOME TO ROOST

CPTC and Caltrans headquarters had developed a working relationship that shared the common goal of offering a solution to the congestion on the 91 and maintaining the safety of cars entering and exiting the toll facility. Then, stunningly, without CPTC's knowledge (and possibly Caltrans headquarters'), Caltrans District 12, overseer of Orange County, issued a

---

[9]Megan Garvey, "91 Express Lanes Pull in a Profit for First Time," *Los Angeles Times*, April 24, 1999 (Orange County Edition).

[10]Caltrans and U.S. Department of Transportation, "Executive Summary," (Senate Transportation Committee Binder), 2.

"study" suggesting the addition of two auxiliary lanes in each direction—essentially restoring the lanes that were dropped to create the toll facility.[11] It looked exactly like the kind of capacity-increasing project that was strictly prohibited under the franchise agreement.

On March 5, 1999, CPTC filed a $100 million lawsuit against Caltrans District 12 in Superior Court in San Diego. "Greg [Hulsizer] heard through the grapevine about the project. District 12 waited a couple months before telling him," grumbled Chris Micheli, who works closely with CPTC. "CPTC has to be notified in advance of safety projects. We can't veto them, but we have to be apprised of them."[12] A study by Wilbur Smith Associates, a traffic consultant for the 91 Express Lanes, found that Caltrans' auxiliary lane project would result in a 40 to 50 percent revenue reduction per year from 2001 to 2015.[13]

From the time of the proposal, Caltrans District 12 had been compiling safety statistics on the 91 Freeway, and they said that the presence of the toll lanes directly contributed to a sharp increase in traffic accidents. When Caltrans safety experts outlined the pattern of accidents along the 91 Freeway, the numbers varied widely. In one 1998 Caltrans report, officials said that accidents increased by 72 percent on the 91 Freeway after the toll lanes opened. In a 1999 report the numbers had risen to 183 percent.[14] In the midst of the litigation, Caltrans spokesperson Jim Drago noted, "We still don't know where the numbers came from. We don't know which of them are correct. We are just trying to come up with numbers we can stand behind."[15]

One Caltrans document in particular caused quite a stir in the litigation process. In a document dated January 14, 1999, Caltrans project engineer Javier Galindo said he was changing the project from a widening for

---

[11]Sharon McNary, "Freeway Still Chokes on Corona," *Press-Enterprise* (Riverside, Calif.), December 5, 1999.

[12]Chris Micheli, personal interview.

[13]Megan Garvey, "Road Owner Sues to Block New 91 Lanes," *Los Angeles Times*, March 6, 1999 (Orange County Edition).

[14]Kimberly Kindy, "Caltrans Botched Road Data," *Orange County Register*, January 27, 2000.

[15]*Ibid.*

capacity to a safety project to "get around the franchise agreement."[16] "The safety project never should have been pushed by the district," noted Roy Nagy, "they got way out of the box on that one."

What had become astonishingly clear was that regional components of Caltrans were still under pressure to reduce congestion by increasing capacity on public roadways as money became available; but maintaining toll road revenues depended on increasing congestion by limiting capacity on public roadways. This was the legacy of AB 680 in more affluent and more congested times.

NEWTRAC AND THE NONPROFIT VARIABLE

With California emerging from the recession and experiencing budget surpluses, it became increasingly evident that the public pressure statewide to add freeway capacity could doom toll roads, particularly with the safety exception to the noncompetition agreement. It could always be argued that congested freeways—with increased air pollution, growing evidence of "road rage," and an inability to reach accident victims—are inherently unsafe. It is quite possible that this reasoning caused what happened next.

During the litigation between Caltrans and CPTC, CPTC executed a letter of intent to sell its toll road holdings to the Southern California Public Transportation Corporation, a nonprofit corporation doing business as NewTrac. CPTC's justification for the sale was that its parent company was divesting a portion of its assets, including the 91 toll road. CPTC projected that NewTrac, utilizing tax-exempt bonds, would return over a half-billion dollars in improvements to the corridor over the next 30 years.[17] A for-profit owner, they argued, would return nothing to the corridor since toll revenues would be devoted to debt service and profit distributions. Both organizations asked Caltrans to approve the deal. However, the

---

[16]*Ibid.*

[17]California Private Transportation Company, L.P. "Briefing: Facts Regarding the 91 Express Lanes and the Proposed Sale Transaction between the California Private Transportation Company and NewTrac," January 21, 2000 (Senate Transportation Committee Binder).

relationship between CPTC and NewTrac triggered speculation by state officials that the transaction was not at "arms-length."[18]

DOMINOES

On October 12, 1999, CPTC and Caltrans settled the litigation regarding proposed improvements. There would be project postponements and downsizing combined with acknowledgment of anticompetitive consequences—the result was a $12 million reduction in NewTrac's purchase price of the 91 express lanes.[19] On October 15, 1999, newly appointed Caltrans Director Jose Medina approved the sale to NewTrac.

Residents who traveled the 91 Freeway felt as if the state had caved in on the lawsuit and ignored the needs of commuters. "Caltrans did a real disservice and injustice to the taxpayers. They backed us up against the wall. We are stuck; we have to live with it. We've been taken advantage of by a state agency," complained Janine Tolly, an Anaheim Hills resident.[20]

In early November, the California Infrastructure and Economic Development Bank approved up to $325 million in tax-exempt state backed

---

[18]The prospect of selling the 91 Express Lanes to a nonprofit entity was not a new idea—it had been presented to the Wilson administration in 1998. Dean Dunphy, the Wilson cabinet member who oversaw Caltrans, had rejected the proposed sale to NewTrac. "(The private company) hand-picked their board before they ever came to us. We needed to appoint some of the members (to the board) so the public interest was protected. It was not an arm's-length relationship. You can't just create these things and bring your buddies in," Dunphy told the *Orange County Register* on December 24. During his tenure, Dunphy blocked Caltrans from writing a letter to the IRS that testified to the public benefits of the sale to NewTrac. This prevented tax-exempt bonds from being issued to finance the acquisition. Although Dunphy supported the concept of private partnerships to reduce traffic congestion, he questioned the public benefit of the sale. "The private sector has got to see this is not a giant rat hole down which you pour money," Dunphy explained the next day in the *Riverside Press Enterprise*. Because of the national attention that the 91 express lanes received, Dunphy's primary concern was that the project be seen as a success in terms of public/private agreements.

[19]Caltrans and CPTC, "Auxiliary Lanes Litigation Settlement Agreement," October 12, 1999.

[20]Janine Tolly, telephone interview, April 10, 2000.

bonds to help NewTrac purchase the toll road—any funding raised above the selling price would be allocated to a reserve to pay for costs associated with the transaction. Standard & Poor's, one of the country's top bond rating firms, gave the lowest investment-grade rating to the toll road bonds, citing concerns about the growth assumptions of NewTrac. In mid-November, NewTrac agreed to buy the 91 Express Lanes.

Despite speculation that CPTC initiated the sale to "bail-out" the project, CPTC insisted that it generated more than $10 million in operating income in 1999, and could earn almost $1 billion in pretax profits for the next 30 years.[21] However, in a December 3 teleconference between prospective bond investors and CPTC, several investors took issue with the income projections for 1999 and noted that the business relationship between NewTrac and CPTC was too close for comfort.

Orrick, Herrington, and Sutcliffe had served as counsel to the California Infrastructure and Economic Development Bank, performed work for CPTC, and then helped NewTrac apply for nonprofit status with the Internal Revenue Service. When NewTrac applied for $274 million in taxpayer-subsidized financing from the EDB, Orrick, Herrington issued a favorable letter for NewTrac, indicating that the company's IRS paperwork was in order.[22]

On December 7, the Riverside County Board of Supervisors voted unanimously to pursue legal action to halt the sale of the toll road. Once the county announced its intentions to sue, Attorney General Bill Lockyer, who had been adamantly opposed to the toll roads while a legislator, launched an investigation.[23] The next day, State Treasurer Phil Angelides postponed the bond sale.[24]

At a legislative hearing, it was clear that the pendulum had again swung against private toll roads,. Even one of the most conservative Republicans, Assemblyman Tom McClintock, who had often argued that business can do

---

[21]CPTC, "Briefing."

[22]James B. Kelleher, Jennifer B. McKim, and Kate Berry, "Single Law Firm Work for All Three Parties in Bond Deal," *Orange County Register*, December 14, 1999.

[23]Megan Garvey and Meg James, "State Taking 'Hard Look' at Road Sale," *Los Angeles Times*, December 8, 1999 (Orange County Edition).

[24]Joint Hearing Assembly Transportation Committee and Senate Transportation Committee: "State Route 91 Expressways," February 1, 2000.

it better, suggested that the state buy the franchise rights and open the lanes to the public: "It's a state-sanctioned monopoly. If we allow it to continue, we are creating a new generation of robber barons." It remains to be seen if California continues its experiment with toll roads and the concept of public/private partnerships. The moral of the tale was told by CPTC General Manager, Greg Hulsizer: "This is bigger than 91. Other investors are watching . . . how the state treats its private [sector]. When you ask the private sector to take a risk, you have to let them reap their reward."